_____

By

_____

On the Occasion of

_____

Date

_____

THE GOLDEN TREASURY OF BIBLE WISDOM

Words of Encouragement, Hope, and Wisdom

BARBOUR
PUBLISHING

Cover image © Image Source
Cover design by Robyn Martins

Published by Barbour Publishing, Inc., P.O. Box 719, Uhrichsville, Ohio 44683, www.barbourbooks.com

Our mission is to publish and distribute inspirational products offering exceptional value and biblical encouragement to the masses.

Published by Barbour Publishing, Inc., P.O. Box 719, Uhrichsville, Ohio 44683, www.barbourbooks.com

 Member of the
Evangelical Christian
Publishers Association

Printed in the United States of America.
5 4 3 2 1

To the kind and courageous publishers and editors, in this and other lands, who have honored the God-given instrument of the printing press by publishing the best news of all, the Word of God, I dedicate this collection.

"The Lord gave the word;
great was the company of those that published it."
—PSALM 68:11

Herschel B. Dean

ACKNOWLEDGMENTS

Since 1952, Rev. H. B. Dean's Bible verse and timely message columns have appeared daily in hundreds of newspapers throughout the United States and in other countries.

Printed under various titles, the works of Herschel Dean truly have been inspired gospel seeds sown in the hearts of many thousands of readers and have been cherished by people from all walks of life.

It is with prayerful gratitude for this servant of God's obedient and dedicated response to the inspiration of the Holy Spirit that we proudly present *The Golden Treasury of Bible Wisdom*.

"For God is not unrighteous to forget your work and labor of love, which ye have shown toward his name."—Hebrews 6:10

The LaMar Publishing Co.

Contents

Words of
Assurance....

Words of Assurance

"And we know that all things work together for good to them that love God, to them who are the called according to his purpose."

Romans 8:28

If you are a believer in Christ, God has everything working for you, though at the moment it may seem to be going against you. Just because we can't see it is no sign that He is not doing it. "If God be for us, who can be against us."

"For I am persuaded, that neither death, nor life, nor angels, nor principalities, nor powers, nor things present, nor things to come, Nor height, nor depth, nor any other creature, shall be able to separate us from the love of God, which is in Christ Jesus our Lord."

Romans 8:38,39

God is trying to get through with the news that you are a winner. Let Him!

"These things I have spoken unto you, that in me ye might have peace. In the world ye shall have tribulation: but be of good cheer; I have overcome the world."

John 16:33

What victory - and to think that we are a part of it. "As my Father hath sent me, even so send I you." Christ in you, the hope of glory. Amen.

"And I will bless them that bless thee, and curse him that curseth thee: and in thee shall all families of the earth be blessed."

Genesis 12:3

What a sweeping promise! What an historical fact - and the end is not yet.

"And he said unto me, My grace is sufficient for thee: for my strength is made perfect in weakness. Most gladly therefore will I rather glory in my infirmities, that the power of Christ may rest upon me."

II Corinthians 12:9

Just when you think it's all over, look for a breath of new life to pick you up. He is all sufficient and yours for the asking. "Behold, I stand at the door and knock: if any man hear my voice, and open the door, I will come in."

"For God so loved the world, that he gave his only begotten Son, that whosoever believeth in him should not perish, but have everlasting life."

John 3:16

If this was the only word we had from God, it would be enough. Put your name in the middle of it and get ready for excitement now and eternal life forever. Thanks, Father, You did it. We believe it.

―――――――――

"Come unto me, all ye that labour and are heavy laden, and I will give you rest."

Matthew 11:28

Here is the invitation to all for rest and reality, but we must take the initiative to realize it.

―――――――――

"He that dwelleth in the secret place of the most High shall abide under the shadow of the Almighty."

Psalms 91:1

As we search for our place in life, may this be the first one that we find. Everything else will fall in line.

―――――――――

"And Hezekiah received the letter of the hand of the messengers, and read it: and Hezekiah went up into the house of the Lord, and spread it before the Lord."

II Kings 19:14

We should be as wise with the burdens of life! Take them before the Lord and leave them there, before they take us under. "He careth for you."

"And I will restore to you the years that the locust hath eaten, the cankerworm, and the caterpillar, and the palmerworm, my great army which I sent among you."

Joel 2:25

If you feel like you have thrown your life to the wind, take a look at the only One who can make you a winner. He is the author of time and can make up for all that's lost. Take Jesus today and watch how quickly He can turn things around for you. Only God can take a life of wasted years and defeat and turn it all into victory. Let Him!

"And it is easier for heaven and earth to pass, than one tittle of the law to fail."

Luke 16:17

The Lord has never been known to go back on His Word or back down on His promises. "Only believe."

"There remaineth therefore a rest to the people of God."

Hebrews 4:9

Only God's people can rest assured. "Come unto me, all ye that labour and are heavy laden, and I will give you rest."

"Behold, I have refined thee, but not with silver; I have chosen thee in the furnace of affliction."

Isaiah 48:10

"The servant is not greater than his lord," and as Jesus was tested in the furnace of affliction and persecution, even so it is the furnace that refines us and makes us fit for real service. But always remember, "He knoweth our frames" and He is our strength in every trial.

"Who shall separate us from the love of Christ?"

Romans 8:35

Many have tried to separate God's people from Him in various ways, but He says, "I will be with him in trouble." Men have hidden out in caves to read the Bible; they have been burned at the stake and thrown to the lions, but God has brought them through it all. "Our anchor holds."

"For I am with thee, and no man shall set on thee to hurt thee: for I have much people in this city."

Acts 18:10

In your darkest hour, remember that He who holds the whole world in the palm of His hand is watching and is able to deliver. "For he shall give his angels charge over thee, to keep thee in all thy ways."

"And they shall be mine, saith the Lord of hosts, in that day when I make up my jewels; and I will spare them, as a man spareth his own son that serveth him."

Malachi 3:17

God has His plans for His people, and through Christ, everyone can be a part of those plans.

_____

"For he shall give his angels charge over thee, to keep thee in all thy ways."

Psalms 91:11

It's a dangerous thing to be on your own and away from God. Doubtless we would shudder and rejoice if we could see the Lord working behind the scenes of our lives keeping us from the many dangers that fall across our path.

_____

"Behold, the Lord's hand is not shortened, that it cannot save; neither his ear heavy, that it cannot hear."

Isaiah 59:1

No matter how far down or how high up you are, the hand of God can reach you. No one is out of reach. No one need be out of touch with the Lord.

———————

"His mother saith unto the servants, Whatsoever he saith unto you, do it."

John 2:5

You can proceed on His promise and move with confidence at His command. The miraculous is waiting for those who dare to take the Lord at His Word.

———————

"And he prayed again, and the heaven gave rain, and the earth brought forth her fruit."

James 5:18

Here is the story of a man who, through faith and prayer, opened up Heaven. He is not in a class by himself. "These signs shall follow them that believe." Heaven will still open to those who approach it on the Lord's terms. "If ye shall ask anything in my name, I will do it."

———————

"There hath no temptation taken you but such as is common to man: but God is faithful, who will not suffer you to be tempted above that ye are able; but will with the temptation also make a way to escape, that ye may be able to bear it."
I Corinthians 10:13

Life is filled with a lot of subtle temptations that surrender only to the supernatural. "The Lord knoweth how to deliver the godly out of temptations."

───────────

"But will God in very deed dwell with men on the earth? . . ."
II Chronicles 6:18

The greatest privilege of a Christian is that he enjoys the presence of the Lord now. "I will never leave thee, nor forsake thee."

───────────

"Because thou hast made the Lord, which is my refuge, even the most High, thy habitation; There shall no evil befall thee, neither shall any plague come nigh thy dwelling."
Psalms 91:9,10

Every believer has the right to claim this promise and live with confidence that God will keep His Word as we embrace the condition.

───────────

"Blessed be the Lord, that hath given rest unto his people Israel, according to all that he promised: there hath not failed one word of all his good promise, which he promised by the hand of Moses his servant."

I Kings 8:56

Look at the record and leave the rest to Him. He will keep His Word with you. We are but to claim it.

"Commit thy way unto the Lord; trust also in him; and he shall bring it to pass."

Psalms 37:5

God hears and remembers well. Simply turn it over to Him once, and see what happens.

"And he answered, Fear not: for they that be with us are more than they that be with them. And Elisha prayed, and said, Lord, I pray thee, open his eyes, that he may see. And the Lord opened the eyes of the young man; and he saw: and, behold, the mountain was full of horses and chariots of fire round about Elisha."

II Kings 6:16,17

Think miracles! God has everything under control. Keep your eyes on Him and not on the circumstances. "Fear thou not; for I am with thee . . ."

"For as the rain cometh down, and the snow from heaven, and returneth not thither, but watereth the earth, and maketh it bring forth and bud, that it may give seed to the sower, and bread to the eater: So shall my word be that goeth forth out of my mouth: it shall not return unto me void, but it shall accomplish that which I please, and it shall prosper in the thing whereto I sent it."

Isaiah 55:10,11

Stay in there with the pure Word of God whoever you are and wherever you are. Whether you see it fulfilled the next day or in the next life, there is nothing but success and victory waiting for you. Father, thank You for Your faithful Word.

"The Spirit itself beareth witness with our spirit, that we are the children of God."
Romans 8:16

It's the harmony of our spirit and God's Spirit that bears testimony as to whether or not our hearts are right and we are His. If there is a trace of doubt, turn to Jesus now and clear it up while there is time.

"He is not here: for he is risen, as he said. Come, see the place where the Lord lay."
Matthew 28:6

He is alive and "at the right hand of the Father ever living to make intercession for us." "Because I live, ye shall live also." Thank You, Father, for the resurrection of Jesus, Your Son, and our assurance of eternal life through Him.

"Beloved, I wish above all things that thou mayest prosper and be in health, even as thy soul prospereth."

III John 2

God wants us to believe for the best in all things, for He surely means for us to have them. "If ye shall ask anything in my name, I will do it."

———————————

"I delight to do thy will, O my God."
Psalms 40:8

Be willing for God to have His way and, though everything seems to go wrong, in the end you will see that God was right. "All things work together for good to them that love God, to them who are the called according to his purpose."

———————————

"Peace I leave with you, my peace I give unto you: not as the world giveth, give I unto you. Let not your heart be troubled, neither let it be afraid."

John 14:27

About all the world has to offer is temporary tranquilizers in one form or another to keep the mind off the condition of the heart. Trust Christ for real peace of mind and heart.

"Be still, and know that I am God: I will be exalted among the heathen, I will be exalted in the earth."

Psalms 46:10

In an age of haste, it is good to remember that there is yet a lot to be learned and accomplished in the art of just waiting. Wait on the Lord and He shall renew thy strength.

"The Lord is my light and my salvation; whom shall I fear? the Lord is the strength of my life; of whom shall I be afraid?"

Psalms 27:1

The man who walks with God doesn't have to run from anything. "Fear thou not; for I am with thee."

". . . Death is swallowed up in victory. O death, where is thy sting? O grave, where is thy victory?"

I Corinthians 15:54,55

Death is not a dead end but a doorway. Jesus said, "He that believeth on me, though he were dead, yet shall he live."

———————

"And we know that all things work together for good to them that love God, to them who are the called according to his purpose."

Romans 8:28

God has a way of making things come out right for those who love Him and serve Him. "No good thing will he withhold from them that walk uprightly."

———————

"Ye are of God, little children, and have overcome them: because greater is he that is in you, than he that is in the world."

I John 4:4

We come to master the problems from without when we learn to appropriate power from within. "Nothing shall be impossible unto you."

———————

"There hath no temptation taken you but such as is common to man: but God is faithful, who will not suffer you to be tempted above that ye are able; but will with the temptation also make a way to escape, that ye may be able to bear it."

I Corinthians 10:13

God walks in the midst of all the trials of His children with outstretched hands of answers and assurance. He is our Guide who knows the way out; you can trust Him.

———————

"There remaineth therefore a rest to the people of God."

Hebrews 4:9

Only the people of God can rest assured.

———————

"He answered and said, Lo, I see four men loose, walking in the midst of the fire, and they have no hurt; and the form of the fourth is like the Son of God."

Daniel 3:25

In every fiery trial of life, the child of God can expect the presence of the Saviour to see him through.

———————

"Thou shalt not be afraid for the terror by night; nor for the arrow that flieth by day."
Psalms 91:5

Our gracious Lord has provided for our protection, as well as our pardon. "Be not afraid, only believe."

―――――――――

"Blessed is the nation whose God is the Lord."
Psalms 33:12

If God is in the government, faith will be in the people. A nation under God will never be under another power.

―――――――――

"What shall we then say to these things? If God be for us, who can be against us?"
Romans 8:31

God with us is not always a good sign that man is for us, but "greater is he that is in you than he that is in the world."

―――――――――

"Happy is he that hath the God of Jacob for his help, whose hope is in the Lord his God."
Psalms 146:5

If you have the Lord on your side, the world can stand on its head and you can still remain calm.

––––––––––

"These things have I written unto you that believe on the name of the Son of God; that ye may know that ye have eternal life, and that ye may believe on the name of the Son of God."
I John 5:13

Salvation through Christ carries with it a guaranteed future in Heaven and a wonderful life while on earth.

––––––––––

"Because thou hast made the Lord, which is my refuge, even the most High, thy habitation; There shall no evil befall thee, neither shall any plague come nigh thy dwelling."
Psalms 91:9,10

Living with God, and for Him, has a lot of built-in benefits that we can't afford to be without. "My presence shall go with you. . ." "If God be for us, who can be against us?"

––––––––––

"Many are the afflictions of the righteous: but the Lord delivereth him out of them all."

Psalms 34:19

The people of God are not immune to problems, but escorted through them. "If God be for us, who can be against us." "I am with you." Thanks, Lord!

———————

"I can do all things through Christ which strengtheneth me."

Philippians 4:13

Get a picture of Christ in you and develop it by reading and believing this promise. You are in for some living that will surprise you.

———————

"I have set the Lord always before me: because he is at my right hand, I shall not be moved."

Psalms 16:8

No matter how things look, keep your eyes on the Lord. He can bring miracles out of mistakes.

———————

"Thou art my hiding place; thou shalt preserve me from trouble; thou shalt compass me about with songs of deliverance. Selah."

Psalms 32:7

Everything we need, He is. God forgive us for our failure to see this truth. You will never relive today. Make it a good one with God's help.

———————————

"I will both lay me down in peace, and sleep: for thou, Lord, only makest me dwell in safety."

Psalms 4:8

Rest assured, God is wide awake. "The angel of the Lord encampeth round about them that fear him."

———————————

"So that we may boldly say, The Lord is my helper, and I will not fear what man shall do unto me."

Hebrews 13:6

When you think of what you have going for you, how can you let anything get you down? "Fear not, I am with you" - Jesus!

———————————

"And it shall come to pass in the last days, saith God, I will pour out of my Spirit upon all flesh: and your sons and your daughters shall prophesy, and your young men shall see visions, and your old men shall dream dreams: And on my servants and on my handmaidens I will pour out in those days of my Spirit; and they shall prophesy."

Acts 2:17,18

We are living in the midst of these days and the demonstration of God's mighty power around the world is ample proof. "The promise is unto you."

"Behold, I will gather them out of all countries, whither I have driven them in mine anger, and in my fury, and in great wrath; and I will bring them again unto this place, and I will cause them to dwell safely: . . . And I will give them one heart, and one way, that they may fear me for ever, for the good of them, and of their children after them."

Jeremiah 32:37,39

He will keep His Word! He has kept His Word! "Heaven and earth shall pass away, but my words shall not pass away."

"And he said, Abba, Father, all things are possible unto thee; take away this cup from me: nevertheless not what I will, but what thou wilt."

Mark 14:36

We sometimes fear the will of God as though He has forgotten something. He is mindful, merciful and has never made a mistake and is working all things out for our good and His glory. We praise Thee, O God.

"He will bless them that fear the Lord, both small and great. The Lord shall increase you more and more, you and your children."

Psalms 115:13,14

What a promise! Claim it! The Lord is not slack concerning His promise. "Heaven and earth shall pass away, but my words shall not pass away."

"And if I go and prepare a place for you, I will come again, and receive you unto myself; that where I am, there ye may be also."

John 14:3

Don't get too earthbound! This good Word from the Lord, Himself, makes it clear that He is coming again to receive those for whom He has prepared a wonderful place. Now to make sure you are going to make it, simply acknowledge your need and invite Him to come into your heart. "Him that cometh to me I will in no wise cast out."

"Remember me, O my God, concerning this, and wipe not out my good deeds that I have done for the house of my God, and for the offices thereof."

Nehemiah 13:14

The Lord has a long memory and many rewards for the faithful. Stay in there with the work of God and the servant of God. "He shall in no wise lose his reward."

The Bible....

The Bible

"Thy word is a lamp unto my feet, and a light unto my path."

Psalms 119:105

The Word of the Lord was meant to be used by men in travel from earth to Heaven. Perhaps the reason we have run into so many dark and gloomy roads along the way is because we have not recognized it.

"And the Lord appeared again in Shiloh: for the Lord revealed himself to Samuel in Shiloh by the word of the Lord."

I Samuel 3:21

The Bible is God's way of revealing Himself. "Faith cometh by hearing, and hearing by the word of God." Build your faith. Spend more time in your Father's book.

"And Jesus answered him, saying, It is written, That man shall not live by bread alone, but by every word of God."

Luke 4:4

Man needs something more than the products of his own hands in this life and in the life to come.

"The grass withereth, the flower fadeth: but the word of our God shall stand for ever."
Isaiah 40:8

Long after the Bible's critics are dead and buried, the Word of God will still be standing. "Thy word is truth."

———————

"And it is easier for heaven and earth to pass, than one tittle of the law to fail."
Luke 16:17

The Word of God has buried its critics and still marches on as conqueror and comforter, spreading its light to the darkest corners of the earth. "Thy word is truth."

———————

"But the word of God grew and multiplied."
Acts 12:24

This has been the history of the Word of God and this is its future. The truly wise will keep on sharing it faithfully and quickly. "My word will not return unto me void."

———————

"And he said unto them, Full well ye reject the commandment of God, that ye may keep your own tradition . . . Making the word of God of none effect through your tradition, which ye have delivered: and many such like things do ye."
Mark 7:9,13

A lot of people are still trying to pass off their "good old tradition" for the Old Time Gospel. It wouldn't work then, nor will it work now. "Search the scriptures . . ."

———

"But thou, Bethlehem Ephratah, though thou be little among the thousands of Judah, yet out of thee shall he come forth unto me that is to be ruler in Israel; whose goings forth have been from of old, from everlasting."
Micah 5:2

The amazing accuracy of prophecy already fulfilled should make us avid readers of the Bible . . . God's timepiece of what is yet to be.

———

"Ever learning, and never able to come to the knowledge of the truth."
II Timothy 3:7

One of the great tragedies of our time is that most of it is spent in learning error and dodging truth. "Thy word is truth."

―――――――

"And take the helmet of salvation, and the sword of the Spirit, which is the word of God."
Ephesians 6:17

We are to take God's Word to heart, while holding it forth as the world's only hope. Have you read the Bible today - have you shared it with someone? "My words shall not pass away."

―――――――

"Hold fast the form of sound words, which thou hast heard of me, in faith and love which is in Christ Jesus."
II Timothy 1:13

We should keep the Gospel simple, not mystic, and be careful to speak to the present need. There is a danger of belaboring the Scripture instead of just delivering it. "Heaven and earth shall pass away: but my words shall not pass away."

―――――――

"And Jesus answered him, saying, It is written, That man shall not live by bread alone, but by every word of God."

Luke 4:4

A life dependent only on the physical and material is in for some lean times . . . but if the Spiritual intake of His Word has equal time with the physical, we can count on some strong bodies and great Christians.

―――――

"There is a way which seemeth right unto a man, but the end thereof are the ways of death."

Proverbs 14:12

Don't look at the way you feel, but to the Word of God. "Thy word is a lamp unto my feet, and a light unto my path."

―――――

"Whoso despiseth the word shall be destroyed: but he that feareth the commandment shall be rewarded."

Proverbs 13:13

God is watching our reaction to His Word. Have you heard or read any of it lately? Our reward or rebuke is based on how we regard it.

―――――

"Heaven and earth shall pass away: but my words shall not pass away."

Mark 13:31

Long after man has had his say, the Word of God will still be standing. In view of this, we ought to spend more time with it.

"For ever, O Lord, thy word is settled in heaven."

Psalms 119:89

The Word of God has been proofread in Heaven, and its promises are ready for everyone on earth. Read and believe. He will not go back on His Word.

"For the prophecy came not in old time by the will of man: but holy men of God spake as they were moved by the Holy Ghost."

II Peter 1:21

When you read the Bible, remember this. Here is the reason it is so powerful and lasting. "My word shall not pass away . . . It will not return unto me void."

"If any man will do his will, he shall know of the doctrine, whether it be of God, or whether I speak of myself."

John 7:17

The Bible has stood the test of time and talents, and it still marches on bringing release and peace to all who will obey its instructions. "Heaven and earth shall pass away, but my words shall not pass away."

———————

"Thy word have I hid in mine heart, that I might not sin against thee."

Psalms 119:11

Take His Word to heart. It points the way to the abundant life and eternal life.

———————

". . . for great is the wrath of the Lord that is kindled against us, because our fathers have not hearkened unto the words of this book, to do according unto all that which is written concerning us."

II Kings 22:13

Every generation will rise and answer for its neglect of the "Book of Books."

———————

"And the gospel must first be published among all nations."

Mark 13:10

The Gospel is the only guide capable of leading the world out of the darkness and into the marvelous light of Christ. "It is the power of God unto salvation."

". . . thy word is truth."

John 17:17

Trust the word of man and you get what man can do. Trust the Word of God and you get what God has promised. He is able to do the exceeding and the abundant above all that we can ask or think.

"Study to shew thyself approved unto God, a workman that needeth not to be ashamed, rightly dividing the word of truth."

II Timothy 2:15

A person should not only study the Bible for what they can get out of it, but for what it can get out of them.

"Be ye therefore very courageous to keep and to do all that is written in the book of the law of Moses, that ye turn not aside therefrom to the right hand or to the left."

Joshua 23:6

More time with the greatest book on earth will mean better times for all of us. Jesus said, "Heaven and earth shall pass away, but my words shall not pass away."

"Behold, the days come, saith the Lord God, that I will send a famine in the land, not a famine of bread, nor a thirst for water, but of hearing the words of the Lord: And they shall wander from sea to sea, and from the north even to the east, they shall run to and fro to seek the word of the Lord, and shall not find it."

Amos 8:11,12

God has given a gift and left a gift - His Son and His Word. Treat it with reverence, read it with diligence. Some day it will be scarce and man will be hungry for it.

"Be not thou therefore ashamed of the testimony of our Lord . . . but be thou partaker of the afflictions of the gospel according to the power of God.''

II Timothy 1:8

People who are bent on taking the Bible out of public life would be just as happy if they didn't have to face it from the pulpit. Jesus said, "If ye are ashamed of me and my words . . . I will be ashamed of you before my Father and the holy angels.''

"For ever, O Lord, thy word is settled in heaven.''

Psalms 119:89

His Word is everlasting and never failing. We ought to give more heed to it.

"With my whole heart have I sought thee: O let me not wander from thy commandments.''

Psalms 119:10

The Bible is a map to peace, happiness, and Heaven. Follow it and you will have a safe journey. Wander from it and you are in trouble. Discover God in His Word.

"So then faith cometh by hearing, and hearing by the word of God."

Romans 10:17

People who want to have more faith ought to be more faithful in reading the Word of God. "Thy word is a lamp unto my feet, and a light unto my path."

"On that night could not the king sleep, and he commanded to bring the book of records of the chronicles; and they were read before the king."

Esther 6:1

The reading of the Old Book will still settle a lot of nerves and point humanity to a land where strife and tears are strangers.

"Whoso despiseth the word shall be destroyed: but he that feareth the commandment shall be rewarded."

Proverbs 13:13

Respect His Word. Someday you will be judged by it. Use it today as a release of God's power. "The words that I speak unto you, they are spirit, and they are life."

"For the prophecy came not in old time by the will of man: but holy men of God spake as they were moved by the Holy Ghost."

II Peter 1:21

The inspired Word inspires us. That's why we should spend more time with it. Make Bible reading a must. "Faith cometh by hearing, and hearing by the word of God."

"Blessed is he that readeth, and they that hear the words of this prophecy, and keep those things which are written therein: for the time is at hand."

Revelation 1:3

This is another admonition to read God's Word. If we only knew the benefits of the Bible, nothing could keep us from it. "Thy word is truth."

"In God will I praise his word: in the Lord will I praise his word."

Psalms 56:10

One of the great failures of our time is that we have put too much emphasis on man's word and too little emphasis on the Word of God. "The word of the Lord endureth forever."

"But he answered and said, It is written, Man shall not live by bread alone, but by every word that proceedeth out of the mouth of God."

Matthew 4:4

No wonder life gets to be so dull with just a steady diet of what the world has to offer. Build up your faith, brighten up your living. Read a portion of the Word of God daily.

"So then faith cometh by hearing, and hearing by the word of God."

Romans 10:17

To increase your faith, increase your intake of the Word by hearing, reading and praying it. Dear Holy Spirit, read the Word of God through us and help us to retain It in our hearts for the glory of God and in Jesus' name. Amen.

———

"Heaven and earth shall pass away, but my words shall not pass away."

Matthew 24:35

The Word of God is going to stand. Shouldn't we spend more time with It? "The word of the Lord endureth forever."

———

"Then they that feared the Lord spake often one to another: and the Lord hearkened, and heard it, and a book of remembrance was written before him for them that feared the Lord, and that thought upon his name. And they shall be mine, saith the Lord of hosts, in that day when I make up my jewels; and I will spare them, as a man spareth his own son that serveth him."

Malachi 3:16,17

Here is a unique and beautiful bond between believers that should be marked by constant fellowship. To neglect it is an invitation to some lean times in our spiritual lives that are often hard to recover.

———

"Keep therefore the words of this covenant, and do them, that ye may prosper in all that ye do."

Deuteronomy 29:9

Far from being a dry book, the Bible is a guide to all that we have dreamed of. Read a little of it every day and long after you have read, it will be back to bless you. "Thy word have I hid in mine heart, that I might not sin against thee."

———

Faith....

Faith

"... the victory that overcometh the world, even our faith."

I John 5:4

Overcoming faith! That is the need of the hour. Not only faith to start on, but faith to stand on. Faith that is good enough to live by is good enough to die by. "Lord increase our faith."

"And the hand of the Lord was with them: and a great number believed, and turned unto the Lord."

Acts 11:21

In order to have His hand with you, it is absolutely necessary to leave all in His hand. When God is with us, people will believe, and when they believe, they will turn to the Lord. "Let the beauty of Jesus be seen in me."

"Yea, though I walk through the valley of the shadow of death, I will fear no evil: for thou art with me; thy rod and thy staff they comfort me."

Psalms 23:4

The man who has put his faith in God will not be afraid of the future. "Have faith in God."

"If thou canst believe, all things are possible to him that believeth."

Mark 9:23

Daring Christians are a delight to the Lord.

"Not my will, but thine, be done."
Luke 22:42

God knows best and He will do what is best. He is our advocate; trust His judgment. "Without faith it is impossible to please God."

". . . a man full of leprosy: who seeing Jesus fell on his face, and besought him, saying, Lord, if thou wilt, thou canst make me clean. And he put forth his hand, and touched him, saying, I will: be thou clean. And immediately the leprosy departed from him."

Luke 5:12,13

With the acknowledgement that something was wrong came the assurance that there was One who could make it right. "I will: be thou clean."

"And looking round about upon them all, he said unto the man, Stretch forth thy hand. And he did so: and his hand was restored whole as the other."

Luke 6:10

Blessed is the man who obeys the voice of Jesus and believes Him for the inexplainable and the impossible. Believe only. "He is able."

"But without faith it is impossible to please him: for he that cometh to God must believe that he is, and that he is a rewarder of them that diligently seek him."

Hebrews 11:6

Faith takes the strain out of life and the suspense out of eternity. God give us faith to remove mountains and grace to look over the little hills.

———————

"And Simon answering said unto him, Master, we have toiled all the night, and have taken nothing: nevertheless at thy word I will let down the net. And when they had this done, they inclosed a great multitude of fishes: and their net brake."

Luke 5:5,6

Jesus didn't go to where the fish were necessarily, but to where the faith was. He will honor our faith and obedience.

———————

"When Jesus saw their faith, he said unto the sick of the palsy, Son, thy sins be forgiven thee."

Mark 2:5

Apparently God honors the faith of the believer in the behalf of those who have none. A religion of ritual and works can wear you out. A faith that believes God for anything can lift you up. "Without faith it is impossible to please him."

———————

". . . Lord, if it be thou, bid me come unto thee on the water . . . he walked on the water, to go to Jesus."

Matthew 14:28,29

When we step out on faith, the Lord will give us something to stand on. "Faith is the victory that overcomes the world." "Only believe."

"But my God shall supply all your need according to his riches in glory by Christ Jesus."

Philippians 4:19

He supplies what we believe Him for; not what we wish for. Have faith in God. He is able.

"And I say unto you, Ask, and it shall be given you; seek, and ye shall find; knock, and it shall be opened unto you."

Luke 11:9

Here is a formula that puts our faith to work in getting what we need and what He wants us to have. Pray on! Believe only!

"And all things, whatsoever ye shall ask in prayer, believing, ye shall receive."

Matthew 21:22

Go for a miracle. "All things are possible to him that believeth." Lord, we believe!

"So the father knew that it was at the same hour, in the which Jesus said unto him, Thy son liveth. and himself believed, and his whole house."

John 4:53

The Lord needs to only say the word and wonders appear. He has spoken. Let us believe what He said . . . and is saying to us now. "Believe only."

"If ye abide in me, and my words abide in you, ye shall ask what ye will, and it shall be done unto you."

John 15:7

This does not call for a constant "tug of war" striving and struggling, but a simple natural trust as we release our faith to the Father in the name of Jesus. In so doing, we appropriate what He has already provided. Praise His name for it!

"Even so faith, if it hath not works, is dead, being alone."

James 2:17

Faith becomes effective when it becomes active. Take it out of the talking and thinking stage and put it to work practically, quickly and prayerfully. "God hath dealt to every man the measure of faith . . ." It is enough . . . use it!

"When the even was come, they brought unto him many that were possessed with devils: and he cast out the spirits with his word, and healed all that were sick: That it might be fulfilled which was spoken by Esaias the prophet, saying, Himself took our infirmities, and bare our sicknesses."

Matthew 8:16,17

The ministry of Jesus was one of action and authority. He has passed on to all believers that same boldness if we will but see it and use it. He said, "The works that I do shall he do also . . . and greater . . ."

"For verily I say unto you, That whosoever shall say unto this mountain, Be thou removed, and be thou cast into the sea; and shall not doubt in his heart, but shall believe that those things which he saith shall come to pass; he shall have whatsoever he saith.''

Mark 11:23

Do what Jesus said. Speak to your mountains. They have done the talking long enough. "For with God nothing shall be impossible."

''And this is the confidence that we have in him, that, if we ask anything according to his will, he heareth us: And if we know that he hear us, whatsoever we ask, we know that we have the petitions that we desired of him.''

I John 5:14,15

Many find things in His Word and start wondering if it's for them. Don't be looking for conditions but compassion. Take Him at His Word. He has "magnified His Word above His name."

"Verily, verily, I say unto you, He that believeth on me, the works that I do shall he do also; and greater works than these shall he do; because I go unto my Father. And whatsoever ye shall ask in my name, that will I do, that the Father may be glorified in the Son. If ye shall ask any thing in my name, I will do it."

John 14:12-14

Release your faith with me as we look to the Father. Jesus, I take You at Your Word and believe now that multitudes will be saved, believers filled with the Holy Spirit, others healed, and needs met in every part of their lives in Your Name and for the glory of God, Amen.

———————

"And Caleb stilled the people before Moses, and said, Let us go up at once, and possess it; for we are well able to overcome it."

Numbers 13:30

Don't you like to hear someone who follows a negative report with some straight forward talk expressing a God-given faith? You be that person. Believe God for anything. Speak your faith and He will surely come through.

———————

"And the Lord said, If ye had faith as a grain of mustard seed, ye might say unto this sycamine tree, Be thou plucked up by the root, and be thou planted in the sea; and it should obey you."

Luke 17:6

Spoken faith is a mighty force capable of bringing to pass what appears to be the impossible. Dare to believe God for anything. Father, we believe You for great miracles in Jesus' name. Amen.

―――――――――

"By faith the walls of Jericho fell down, after they were compassed about seven days."

Hebrews 11:30

There is no wall thick enough or armed enough to stand against one seed of faith. On with the march. Faith, praise, power and obedience will see the walls down and the windows of Heaven open. Praise God!

―――――――――

"And they said among themselves, Who shall roll us away the stone from the door of the sepulchre? And when they looked, they saw that the stone was rolled away: for it was very great."
Mark 16:3,4

Like us, we anticipate blockades that have long since been removed. Get rid of that negative thinking and nothing shall be impossible unto you. "Believe only."

"And Jesus said unto them, Because of your unbelief: for verily I say unto you, If ye have faith as a grain of mustard seed, ye shall say unto this mountain, Remove hence to yonder place; and it shall remove; and nothing shall be impossible unto you."
Matthew 17:20

Take another look at this and never again make little of your faith, no matter how small it may look to you. It is mountain moving. Use it and a miracle is in the making.

"And he said unto them, Why are ye so fearful? how is it that ye have no faith?"
Mark 4:40

God must stand amazed at our lack of belief in a world of miracles.

————————

"If ye shall ask anything in my name, I will do it."

John 14:14

Answered prayer yields to the bold approach and daring faith. "All things are possible to him that believeth." "He is able."

————————

"For with God nothing shall be impossible."

Luke 1:37

What the world needs is more mustard seed faith to remove manmade mountains. "According to your faith, so be it unto you."

————————

"The Lord shall preserve thy going out and thy coming in from this time forth, and even for evermore."

Psalms 121:8

Our gracious Father gives direction and protection to those who follow in faith. "I am with you."

————————

"And he took him by the right hand, and lifted him up: and immediately his feet and ankle bones received strength. And he leaping up stood, and walked, and entered with them into the temple, walking, and leaping, and praising God."

Acts 3:7, 8

If our faith is up-to-date, you can be sure that the days of miracles are not past. "I am the Lord thy God, I change not."

"Cast not away therefore your confidence, which hath great recompence of reward."

Hebrews 10:35

If you have earnestly prayed about it and have the conviction that what you are doing is right, the Lord will furnish the courage to see you through. "Only believe."

". . . our God is able . . ."

Daniel 3:17

There is no limit to what the Lord will do in answer to daring faith. "With God nothing shall be impossible."

"But without faith it is impossible to please him: for he that cometh to God must believe that he is, and that he is a rewarder of them that diligently seek him."

Hebrews 11:6

The man who truly walks by faith will not run the risk of being embarrassed. "Have faith in God."

"Yea, though I walk through the valley of the shadow of death, I will fear no evil: for thou art with me; thy rod and thy staff they comfort me."

Psalms 23:4

The man who has put his faith in God will not be afraid of the future. "Have faith in God."

"And he said to the woman, Thy faith hath saved thee; go in peace."

Luke 7:50

Put up whatever faith you have and He will match it. Then look for miracles. "God hath given to every man the measure of faith." Use it!

"Say to them that are of a fearful heart, Be strong, fear not: behold, your God will come with vengeance, even God with a recompence; he will come and save you."

Isaiah 35:4

When fear comes calling, turn up the volume of your faith. "Fear thou not for I am with thee . . . I will uphold thee with the right hand of my righteousness."

"For I say, through the grace given unto me, to every man that is among you, not to think of himself more highly than he ought to think; but to think soberly, according as God hath dealt to every man the measure of faith."

Romans 12:3

Don't pray for more faith. Use what you have and watch it multiply. "According to your faith, so be it unto you."

"For God hath not given us the spirit of fear; but of power, and of love, and of a sound mind."

II Timothy 1:7

Turn your fears back with your faith. "God hath not given us the spirit of fear," but He has given us a measure of faith. It is enough. It is mountain moving. "Thy faith hath made thee whole." "Praise God from whom all blessings flow."

"By faith Abraham, when he was called to go out into a place which he should after receive for an inheritance, obeyed; and he went out, not knowing whither he went."

Hebrews 11:8

If we take the first step of faith, it won't be too long until we see that we are not alone. "I will never leave thee nor forsake thee." The big word is obey. The big fact is that He loves us and has plans for our lives.

Family....

Family

"For if ye turn again unto the Lord, your brethren and your children shall find compassion before them that lead them captive, so that they shall come again into this land: for the Lord your God is gracious and merciful, and will not turn away his face from you, if ye return unto him."

II Chronicles 30:9

As a nation, family, church, or individual, so much depends on the direction we take. Start here - "As for me and my house, we will serve the Lord."

"For how shall I go up to my father, and the lad be not with me?"

Genesis 44:34

In our great anxiety to see that our children won't miss anything, we should be super-careful that they don't miss the spiritual. Lead them to God, and take them to church. Forever you will be glad.

". . . Do not sin against the child."

Genesis 42:22

To deprive a child of a Christian home and Christian training is to sin against the child. Failure to convert them and failure to love them is to sin against them. Do not fail to consider the child, lest you find yourself fighting against God and His will.

"But Samuel ministered before the Lord, being a child . . ."

I Samuel 2:18

It doesn't take a grown person to do things for the Lord. He has been able to accomplish a lot more in the lives of many children than in the lives of their parents. "A little child shall lead them."

"Children, obey your parents in all things: for this is well pleasing unto the Lord."

Colossians 3:20

The strained relationship between children and parents can usually be traced to the child's disregard of what the parents have to say and the parents disregard of what God has to say. For a better home life, make it Christ centered.

"Train up a child in the way he should go:
and when he is old, he will not depart from it."
Proverbs 22:6

Some parents seem bent on giving a
child everything but a Christian home. Lead
your child to Christ. Take your child to church!

"For if a man know not how to rule his own
house, how shall he take care of the church of
God?"
I Timothy 3:5

The man who would assume some
authority in God's house ought to be thor-
oughly Christian in his own house.

"There is a generation that curseth their
father, and doth not bless their mother."
Proverbs 30:11

Children who disrespect a good mother
and father automatically incur the displeasure
of Almighty God.

"Now there stood by the cross of Jesus his
mother . . ."
John 19:25

"Mother's prayers have followed you!" If she is still with you and you can't see her in person, whatever it costs, call and express your love to her. I wish I had the privilege.

"Labour not to be rich: cease from thine own wisdom. Wilt thou set thine eyes upon that which is not? for riches certainly make themselves wings; they fly away as an eagle toward heaven."

Proverbs 23:4,5

Before one of you has to leave the other, wouldn't it be wise to invest in that which will always be? If it's all tied up, now is the time to let it loose in the work of the Lord. "Seek ye first the kingdom of God . . ."

"And a man's foes shall be they of his own household."

Matthew 10:36

Since God deals with people individually, don't be discouraged if even your family is without understanding as to what He is telling you - nor be deterred by what they think or say.

"For this child I prayed; and the Lord hath given me my petition which I asked of him: Therefore also I have lent him to the Lord."

I Samuel 1:27,28

Dedicating a child to God is of even more importance than educating him.

"And these words, which I command thee this day, shall be in thine heart: And thou shalt teach them diligently unto thy children, and shalt talk of them when thou sittest in thine house, and when thou walkest by the way, and when thou liest down, and when thou risest up."

Deuteronomy 6:6,7

Do you wonder what is wrong with our children today? We have gotten away from instructing them in God's laws. More of the Word of God should be rehearsed and taught in the home.

"And they said, Believe on the Lord Jesus Christ, and thou shalt be saved, and thy house."

Acts 16:31

Pray on! Believe for the whole house. Father, I join with them in believing for their whole family. Save them by Thy grace, in Jesus' name. Amen.

———————

"But your little ones, which ye said should be a prey, them will I bring in, and they shall know the land which ye have despised."

Numbers 14:31

It is so often the case that God can do more with the children than He can with their parents. "Except ye be converted and become as little children ye shall not enter into the kingdom of heaven."

———————

"And they said, Believe on the Lord Jesus Christ, and thou shalt be saved, and thy house."

Acts 16:31

Take this good word home with you, and ask God to honor it. I will believe with you. Father, on the basis of Your Word which says that "if two of you shall agree on earth as touching anything that they shall ask, it shall be done for them of my Father which is in heaven . . ." I believe with them for the salvation of their family and for any other need that they may have. In Jesus' name, Amen and thank You.

———————

"And all thy children shall be taught of the Lord; and great shall be the peace of thy children."

Isaiah 54:13

Get the child to God and to the Lord's house while there is time. You can be sure that the enemy of all that is good and wholesome will be after them. Don't squander the privilege to worship. Millions before and multitudes now would love the opportunity.

"Train up a child in the way he should go: and when he is old, he will not depart from it."

Proverbs 22:6

Get as much good going as you can quickly! Set some standards; emphasize the spiritual; give the Word of God and the church a place of prominence; and let love be in evidence in the home. God will honor it.

"Every wise woman buildeth her house: but the foolish plucketh it down with her hands."

Proverbs 14:1

Look who is regarded as a great home builder. The good atmosphere that a wife and mother creates around the home is priceless and everlasting. "Mother's prayers have followed you."

Thoughts on Giving....

Thoughts on Giving

"Give, and it shall be given unto you; good measure, pressed down, and shaken together, and running over, shall men give into your bosom. For with the same measure that ye mete withal it shall be measured to you again."

Luke 6:38

A man's security is not in his savings, but in his giving. The Lord loves a cheerful giver.

———————

"The king that faithfully judgeth the poor, his throne shall be established for ever."

Proverbs 29:14

The ministry to the poor lives on forever as one of the greatest tests of sincerity of the human being. "Inasmuch as ye have done it unto one of the least of these my brethren ye have done it unto me."

———————

"And they with whom precious stones were found gave them to the treasure of the house of the Lord . . ."

I Chronicles 29:8

Giving God the leftovers didn't originate with Old Testament giving habits. If they tithed before Christ came, surely we should at least do as much. Quit tipping God and start tithing. "God loves a cheerful giver."

"And Moses returned unto the Lord, and said, Oh, this people have sinned a great sin, and have made them gods of gold."

Exodus 32:31

Humanity has ever been the same. Gold is to be a servant. It is when we elevate it to a god that we are in serious trouble. "The love of money is the root of all evil." If you have means, make them count for the Master.

"But God said unto him, Thou fool, this night thy soul shall be required of thee: then whose shall those things be, which thou hast provided?"

Luke 12:20

People who busy themselves with laying up earthly treasure are apt to discover that it has cost them Heaven. Men ought to use their means in the spread of the Gospel, in the winning of the lost.

"Bring ye all the tithes into the storehouse, that there may be meat in mine house, and prove me now herewith, saith the Lord of hosts, if I will not open you the windows of heaven, and pour you out a blessing, that there shall not be room enough to receive it."

Malachi 3:10

Ten percent of our income belongs to God and He has ways of seeing that we pay it. "Give, and it shall be given unto you . . ."

"For whosoever will save his life shall lose it: but whosoever will lose his life for my sake, the same shall save it."

Luke 9:24

Live miserly with your life and your means and, no matter what you have in the end, you will die a poor failure.

"And all the tithe of the land, whether of the seed of the land, or of the fruit of the tree, is the Lord's: it is holy unto the Lord."

Leviticus 27:30

Is ten percent of what He has given you too much to ask for the work that you claim, as a Christian, to be the most important thing on earth? Try tithing for one month and see the miracle of it all.

———————

"Heal the sick, cleanse the lepers, raise the dead, cast out devils: freely ye have received, freely give."

Matthew 10:8

Learn to be generous with what God has given you. You can't outgive the Lord. "Give, and it shall be given unto you."

———————

"Cast thy bread upon the waters: for thou shalt find it after many days."

Ecclesiastes 11:1

Forget about knowing the results and attend to the sowing. You will be surprised some day at the power of the Gospel seed you have planted. "My word shall not return unto me void."

———————

"And he called unto him his disciples, and saith unto them, Verily I say unto you, That this poor widow hath cast more in, than all they which have cast into the treasury."

Mark 12:43

This has always been true on the average. The poor people support the work of God, while the wealthy give a few crumbs for the cause of Christ while off in search of some project to exalt their own name above His. Why don't you call your pastor and ask what you can do to really make your means count?

"But whoso hath this world's good, and seeth his brother have need, and shutteth up his bowels of compassion from him, how dwelleth the love of God in him?"

I John 3:17

Here is a question that can only be answered by action. Today, God will use you to help someone in need. See to it that you obey His voice. "Inasmuch as ye have done it unto one of the least of these my brethren, ye have done it unto me."

"Withhold not good from them to whom it is due, when it is in the power of thine hand to do it. Say not unto thy neighbour, Go, and come again, and tomorrow I will give; when thou hast it by thee."

Proverbs 3:27,28

We can get so busy talking spiritual that we neglect to do something practical! The Church could use more Christians in work clothes. Share with some needy person today.

"Upon the first day of the week let every one of you lay by him in store, as God hath prospered him, that there be no gatherings when I come."

I Corinthians 16:2

The Bible calls for the support of the Church and the cause of Christ by systematic giving, persistent praying, and dedicated sharing by those who claim an experience with the Lord.

"And when he looked on him, he was afraid, and said, What is it, Lord? And he said unto him, Thy prayers and thine alms are come up for a memorial before God."

Acts 10:4

Man's greatest strength is in his straight line to Heaven. Keep it busy. The whole bounty of God is waiting to be delivered.

"And this stone, which I have set for a pillar, shall be God's house: and of all that thou shalt give me I will surely give the tenth unto thee."

Genesis 28:22

The faith of every believer ought to be shared by systematic giving and some supernatural living. The more you give, the more you will want to give, and the more you will have to give.

"Blessed is he that considereth the poor: the Lord will deliver him in time of trouble. The Lord will preserve him, and keep him alive; and he shall be blessed upon the earth: and thou wilt not deliver him unto the will of his enemies."

Psalms 41:1,2

Being good to the poor carries with it a powerful promise. Who wouldn't want to have a part in it? "Be ye kind."

"For I was an hungred, and ye gave me no meat: I was thirsty, and ye gave me no drink: I was a stranger, and ye took me not in: naked, and ye clothed me not: sick, and in prison, and ye visited me not."

Matthew 25:42,43

Jesus often appears in the form of neglected and little people, to see if we will do even the simple things as proof of our love and loyalty to Him personally.

"And Amaziah said to the man of God, But what shall we do for the hundred talents which I have given to the army of Israel? And the man of God answered, The Lord is able to give thee much more than this."

II Chronicles 25:9

You will never be able to top God in giving, no matter what it is. "Give and it shall be given unto you . . ."

"Ye are cursed with a curse: for ye have robbed me, even this whole nation. Bring ye all the tithes into the storehouse, that there may be meat in mine house, and prove me now herewith, saith the Lord of hosts, if I will not open you the windows of heaven, and pour you out a blessing, that there shall not be room enough to receive it."

Malachi 3:9,10

Give yourself out of that predicament! "Honor the Lord with thy substance and with the first fruits of all thine increase: so shall thy barns be filled with plenty."

———————

"Lay not up for yourselves treasures upon earth, where moth and rust doth corrupt, and where thieves break through and steal: But lay up for yourselves treasures in heaven, where neither moth nor rust doth corrupt; and where thieves do not break through nor steal."

Matthew 6:19,20

One of the greatest drawbacks to Christianity is the Christian's savings account. The rainy day is here. Give what you can, while you can, to share the Gospel of Christ. Forever, you will be glad.

———————

"There is that scattereth, and yet increaseth; and there is that withholdeth more than is meet, but it tendeth to poverty."

Proverbs 11:24

Our gain is in giving out, not in holding back. "It is more blessed to give than to receive."

"I have shewed you all things, how that so labouring ye ought to support the weak, and to remember the words of the Lord Jesus, how he said, It is more blessed to give than to receive."

Acts 20:35

This may not fit in with our thinking, but it fits in with His planning. Do some giving and watch God.

"He that giveth unto the poor shall not lack: but he that hideth his eyes shall have many a curse."

Proverbs 28:27

People of means should look for opportunities to help the less fortunate, not hide from them. There is a feeling that comes with giving that has no comparison.

"There was a certain rich man, which was clothed in purple and fine linen, and fared sumptuously every day."

Luke 16:19

Here was a man busy "living it up", not knowing that he would shortly be giving it up. Father, help us to turn our resources, including all that we are and all that we have, into something that is real and lasting. In Jesus' name. Amen.

———————

"And Jacob vowed a vow, saying, If God will be with me, and will keep me in this way that I go, and will give me bread to eat, and raiment to put on . . . And this stone, which I have set for a pillar, shall be God's house: and of all that thou shalt give me I will surely give the tenth unto thee."

Genesis 28:20,22

There is something about getting right with God that associates itself with giving.

———————

"For the poor shall never cease out of the land: therefore I command thee, saying, Thou shalt open thine hand wide unto thy brother, to thy poor, and to thy needy, in thy land."

Deuteronomy 15:11

The poor have a special place in the heart of God. Be good to them!

———————

". . . Verily I say unto you, Inasmuch as ye have done it unto one of the least of these my brethren, ye have done it unto me."

Matthew 25:40

Anyone wanting to do the Lord a personal favor can do so with an act of kindness to the least of His children. "Love suffereth long, and is kind."

———————

"And all the tithe of the land, whether of the seed of the land, or of the fruit of the tree, is the Lord's: it is holy unto the Lord."

Leviticus 27:30

Every church ought to be supported by every member giving a minimum of the tithe of their income. "The Lord loveth a cheerful giver."

———————

"Honour the Lord with thy substance, and with the firstfruits of all thine increase."

Proverbs 3:9

The work of God is plagued by big talkers and little givers. How can we expect God's best and give crumbs to the cause of Christ? "The tithe is the Lord's."

"I beseech you therefore, brethren, by the mercies of God, that ye present your bodies a living sacrifice, holy, acceptable unto God, which is your reasonable service."

Romans 12:1

We all need to be willing and living sacrifices content in offering ourselves to God. The Lord is not looking for people to die for Him, but to live for Him.

"Whosoever shall seek to save his life shall lose it; and whosoever shall lose his life shall preserve it."

Luke 17:33

The only part of us that we can take with us is what we have given away.

"Blessed is he that considereth the poor: the Lord will deliver him in time of trouble. The Lord will preserve him, and keep him alive; and he shall be blessed upon the earth . . ."

Psalms 41:1,2

The man who has a place in his heart for the unfortunate will be blessed of God and remembered by mankind. You can't out-give God. "Give, and it shall be given unto you."

"I have shewed you all things, how that so labouring you ought to support the weak, and to remember the words of the Lord Jesus, how he said, It is more blessed to give than to receive."

Acts 20:35

Get in on the giving end. That's where God is. You will be the busiest man in town and the most blessed.

"And God is able to make all grace abound toward you; that ye, always having all sufficiency in all things, may abound to every good work."
II Corinthians 9:8

Be looking for places to give to the glory of God, and He will see to it that you have it to give. "God loves a cheerful giver."

———————

"Lay not up for yourselves treasures upon earth, where moth and rust doth corrupt, and where thieves break through and steal: But lay up for yourselves treasures in heaven, where neither moth nor rust doth corrupt, and where thieves do not break through nor steal: For where your treasure is, there will your heart be also."
Matthew 6:19-21

If you are looking for lasting dividends, you had better get something on deposit in Heaven. You can have what you want if you give enough.

———————

"Take heed that ye do not your alms before men, to be seen of them: otherwise ye have no reward of your Father which is in heaven . . . That thine alms may be in secret: and thy Father which seeth in secret himself shall reward thee openly."
Matthew 6:1,4

There are many ways to give, but none is so graceful . . . and harder!

"And he saw also a certain poor widow casting in thither two mites. And he said, Of a truth I say unto you, that this poor widow hath cast in more than they all: For all these have of their abundance cast in unto the offerings of God: but she of her penury hath cast in all the living that she had."

Luke 21:2-4

The Lord still sees the gift and the attitude of the giver. He also knows if you have reached a point of sacrifice in your giving. "The Lord loveth a cheerful giver." Attend your church and give to the cause of Christ through it, and pray for God's servant. He will bless you for it.

"Give, and it shall be given unto you; good measure, pressed down, and shaken together, and running over, shall men give into your bosom. For with the same measure that ye mete withal it shall be measured to you again."

Luke 6:38

We can have what we want if we give enough! Our Father, give us great desire to give of ourselves and our means that we may know the reality of this good Word from You. In Jesus' name. Amen.

". . . I will surely give the tenth unto thee."
Genesis 28:22

Man owes God at least ten percent of his income and all of his life.

"There is that scattereth, and yet increaseth; and there is that withholdeth more than is meet, but it tendeth to poverty. The liberal soul shall be made fat: and he that watereth shall be watered also himself . . . He that diligently seeketh good procureth favour: but he that seeketh mischief, it shall come unto him."

Proverbs 11:24,25,27

This is simply to say that giving does it, whether it is of ourselves or means. Be looking for ways and means to give, to our church first and then to as many worthy projects as possible.

―――――――

"And in my prosperity I said, I shall never be moved."

Psalms 30:6

Look out! The One who gave it can take it away. Father, give us the spirit of generosity, knowing that we cannot outgive You. "Give, and it shall be given unto you."

―――――――

"The king that faithfully judgeth the poor, his throne shall be established for ever."

Proverbs 29:14

Likewise, if we would find favor with God, we should look for some poor people to share His love and our means with.

God's Love....

God's Love

"For God so loved the world, that he gave his only begotten Son, that whosoever believeth in him should not perish, but have everlasting life."

John 3:16

God's love is big enough to cover the world and yet individual enough so that the least of us are included.

"For I am persuaded, that neither death, nor life, nor angels, nor principalities, nor powers, nor things present, nor things to come, Nor height, nor depth, nor any other creature, shall be able to separate us from the love of God, which is in Christ Jesus our Lord."

Romans 8:38,39

He is not only a Saviour, but a keeper. "Thou wilt keep him in perfect peace, whose mind is stayed on thee."

"Hatred stirreth up strifes: but love covereth all sins."

Proverbs 10:12

Love and hatred cannot abide together in the human heart. "By this shall all men know that ye are my disciples, if ye have love one to another." "Love covers a multitude of sins."

"That I may cause those that love me to inherit substance; and I will fill their treasures."
Proverbs 8:21

Once our love and commitment to the Lord is established, there is no end to what He will do for us, and Jesus said, "through us." "But seek ye first the kingdom of God, and his righteousness; and all these things shall be added unto you."

"O righteous Father, the world hath not known thee: but I have known thee, and these have known that thou hast sent me. And I have declared unto them thy name, and will declare it: that the love wherewith thou hast loved me may be in them, and I in them."
John 17:25,26

Look how much we have going for us. We were included in His prayer then. We are included now. "He ever liveth to make intercession for us."

"And the Lord God planted a garden eastward in Eden; and there he put the man whom he had formed."

Genesis 2:8

God, in His love, made man and put him in a garden. Man, in disobedience, hate, and sin, has created a jungle for himself. Only the Lord Jesus knows the way out! He provided it at the cross. "I am the way . . ."

"Let them shout for joy, and be glad, that favour my righteous cause: yea, let them say continually, Let the Lord be magnified, which hath pleasure in the prosperity of his servant."

Psalms 35:27

Whoever heard of a king who wanted to work a hardship on one of his children? The Lord is the King of Kings, and everyone who has accepted His Son is entitled to what He has. He has made the provision, and He takes pleasure in seeing us prosper. Thank You, Lord, for it all.

"He that spared not his own Son, but delivered him up for us all, how shall he not with him also freely give us all things?"

Romans 8:32

Believe big! What you are asking is nothing compared to what He has already given. "Is any thing too hard for the Lord?"

"For the mountains shall depart, and the hills be removed; but my kindness shall not depart from thee, neither shall the covenant of my peace be removed, saith the Lord that hath mercy on thee."

Isaiah 54:10

Look at the words He uses to show that He loves you. Lose your fears and cares in the midst of this great promise.

"And they crucified him, and parted his garments, casting lots: that it might be fulfilled which was spoken by the prophet, They parted my garments among them, and upon my vesture did they cast lots. And sitting down they watched him there."

Matthew 27:35,36

The death of Jesus was fulfilled prophecy, and foretold love. "God so loved . . that he gave."

"For their heart was not right with him, neither were they stedfast in his covenant. But he, being full of compassion, forgave their iniquity, and destroyed them not: yea, many a time turned he his anger away, and did not stir up all his wrath."

Psalms 78:37,38

Isn't God good? In spite of our failings, He is ready to forgive. But remember, He said, "My Spirit will not always strive with man." "Today if ye will hear his voice, harden not your hearts . . ."

"Blessed be the Lord, that hath given rest unto his people Israel, according to all that he promised: there hath not failed one word of all his good promise, which he promised by the hand of Moses his servant."

I Kings 8:56

Look at the record and leave the rest to Him. He will keep His Word with you. We are but to claim it.

"The Lord is gracious, and full of compassion . . . and of great mercy."

Psalms 145:8

He who said, "I have compassion on the multitude" is still interested in solving even the smallest problem. Earth has no sorrow that Heaven cannot heal.

"I, even I, am he that blotteth out thy transgressions for mine own sake, and will not remember thy sins."

Isaiah 43:25

God is not like man, for after we have acknowledged our wrong, He remembers it no longer. To be forgiving is to be Godlike. To forget the past is to be even more like God.

"Casting all your care upon him; for he careth for you."

I Peter 5:7

The Lord will lift your burden if you will let go. Christ cares, but He cannot carry that which we refuse to commit to Him.

". . . Eye hath not seen, nor ear heard, neither have entered into the heart of man, the things which God hath prepared for them that love him."

I Corinthians 2:9

Not only has He prepared the joys of this life for those who love Him, but at the end of our lives here, we will be amazed at what He has for us. Pass up that which seems to glitter in this life, but which in reality is out to rob us of God's best. Then in the end, you will see it was best for Him to have His way with thee.

———————

". . . God be merciful to me a sinner."
Luke 18:13

Because He came to save that which was lost, He cannot do anything for us until we acknowledge our lost condition. Sin may be clasped so close, we cannot see its face.

———————

"What time I am afraid, I will trust in thee."
Psalms 56:3

The love of God sets us free from the fear of man. "Thou art my shield and refuge."

———————

"For God so loved the world, that he gave his only begotten Son, that whosoever believeth in him should not perish, but have everlasting life."

John 3:16

The salvation of man cost God the death of His only Son. It is so unreasonable to think that man can ignore Him and incur the favor of the Father.

"I will say of the Lord, He is my refuge and my fortress: my God; in him will I trust."

Psalms 91:2

He is both a place to hide and abide. Come in out of the storm and strife of life regularly and meet with your Maker. You will be better equipped to face the world and do His work.

"All thy strong holds shall be like fig trees with the firstripe figs: if they be shaken, they shall even fall into the mouth of the eater."

Nahum 3:12

In our rebellion toward God, it is well to remember what would happen if He withdrew His restraining hand of mercy and left us to our enemies.

"If ye then, being evil, know how to give good gifts unto your children, how much more shall your Father which is in heaven give good things to them that ask him?"

Matthew 7:11

We should not only be courageous in our asking, but confident of His answer.

"For I am the Lord, I change not; therefore ye sons of Jacob are not consumed."

Malachi 3:6

It is in our little thinking and lack of faith that the power and grace of God is past tense. Not so. He loves you, has a plan for your life and is the "same yesterday, today and forever."

"For I am persuaded, that neither death, nor life, nor angels, nor principalities, nor powers, nor things present, nor things to come, Nor height, nor depth, nor any other creature, shall be able to separated us from the love of God, which is in Christ Jesus our Lord."

Romans 8:38,39

He is not only a Saviour, but a keeper. "Thou wilt keep him in perfect peace, whose mind is stayed on thee."

". . . the Lord thinketh upon me . . ."
Psalms 40:17

The great and eternal God has me in mind. How can I ignore Him? God said, "I have loved thee with an everlasting love."

"Behold, what manner of love the Father hath bestowed upon us, that we should be called the sons of God: therefore the world knoweth us not, because it knew him not."

I John 3:1

What a present, and what a future for the follower; and thank God, no past. Don't miss such a love!

"Thou hast given him his heart's desire, and hast not withholden the request of his lips. Selah"
Psalms 21:2

The truth about God is that He is waiting and wanting to give. The trouble with us is that we think He has to be talked into it.

———

"For God so loved the world, that he gave his only begotten Son, that whosoever believeth in him should not perish, but have everlasting life."

John 3:16

Here is the whole story of the old, old story. Take it to heart. It will take you to Heaven.

———

"And I will give thee the treasures of darkness, and hidden riches of secret places, that thou mayest know that I, the Lord, which call thee by thy name, am the God of Israel."

Isaiah 45:3

"No good thing will he withhold from them that walk uprightly." Father, guide Your children into all the prosperity that You planned for us spiritually and physically and give us a generous spirit to go with it. In Jesus' dear name. Amen.

"But God commendeth his love toward us, in that, while we were yet sinners, Christ died for us."

Romans 5:8

Long before it was decided which way you were going, Jesus went to the cross to assure you of the abundant and eternal life. "He that believeth on the Son hath everlasting life: and he that believeth not the Son shall not see life . . ."

"The Lord thy God in the midst of thee is mighty; he will save, he will rejoice over thee with joy; he will rest in his love, he will joy over thee with singing."

Zephaniah 3:17

Don't be shaken by what you see and feel. Only consider the One standing by you. "I will never leave thee, nor forsake thee."

"Blessed be the Lord, that hath given rest unto his people Israel, according to all that he promised: there hath not failed one word of all his good promise, which he promised by the hand of Moses his servant."

I Kings 8:56

God's Word is a great deal more than cold print. It is charged with the power of the Holy Ghost to bring into our lives might and miracles such as we have never known.

"Jesus answered and said unto him, If a man love me, he will keep my words: and my Father will love him, and we will come unto him, and make our abode with him."

John 14:23

Behold the reward in the keeping of His Word! "We will come unto him, and make our abode with him." What living . . . what love! "Greater is he that is in you than he that is in the world."

"The Lord thy God in the midst of thee is mighty; he will save, he will rejoice over thee with joy; he will rest in his love, he will joy over thee with singing."

Zephaniah 3:17

Don't ever think that you can stump God with big prayer requests. "Call unto me, and I will answer thee, and show thee great and mighty things, which thou knowest not." Praise God for His mighty acts.

"He that spared not his own Son, but delivered him up for us all, how shall he not with him also freely give us all things?"

Romans 8:32

The love of God that gave us Jesus will not withhold anything else from us that would be for our good and His glory. "Beloved, I wish above all things that thou mayest prosper and be in health, even as thy soul prospereth."

"And he will love thee, and bless thee, and multiply thee: he will also bless the fruit of thy womb, and the fruit of thy land, thy corn, and thy wine, and thine oil, the increase of thy kine, and the flocks of thy sheep, in the land which he sware unto thy fathers to give thee."

Deuteronomy 7:13

What a promise! What a fulfillment! "My word shall not return unto me void."

"Who forgiveth all thine iniquities; who healeth all thy diseases."

Psalms 103:3

All is covered, but we must come. "Come unto me, all ye that labor and are heavy laden, and I will give you rest." Father, touch the hurt and the needs of this reader in this moment. I ask in Jesus' mighty name. Amen.

"But the very hairs of your head are all numbered."

Matthew 10:30

If you are inclined to think that you are unnoticed by the Lord, give this another reading. God loves you and has plans for your life. Ask Him what they are.

"And the very God of peace sanctify you wholly; and I pray God your whole spirit and soul and body be preserved blameless unto the coming of our Lord Jesus Christ. Faithful is he that calleth you, who also will do it."

I Thessalonians 5:23,24

God's grace is sufficient. Give it all over to Him . . . "who are kept by the power of God through faith unto salvation."

"But he giveth more grace. Wherefore he saith, God resisteth the proud, but giveth grace unto the humble."

James 4:6

The humble stand moves the heart of God. "Humble yourselves in the sight of the Lord and he shall lift you up."

"And he said unto me, My grace is sufficient for thee: for my strength is made perfect in weakness. Most gladly therefore will I rather glory in my infirmities, that the power of Christ may rest upon me."

II Corinthians 12:9

When we come to the end of ourselves, it is the beginning of Himself. "If God be for us, who can be against us." Thanks, Lord, that it is not our strength but Yours that sees us through and over.

"He that spared not his own Son, but delivered him up for us all, how shall he not with him also freely give us all things?"

Romans 8:32

This forever settles the issue that nothing is too much to ask of the Lord. If He went that far, and He did, to prove His love, He will go to any length to meet our needs. "Behold, I am the Lord, the God of all flesh: is there anything too hard for me?"

"Not that we are sufficient of ourselves to think any thing as of ourselves; but our sufficiency is of God."

II Corinthians 3:5

God is enough! He is the source of all that is good . . . and "No good thing will he withhold from them that walk uprightly." "My grace is sufficient for thee."

"And will be a Father unto you, and ye shall be my sons and daughters, saith the Lord Almighty."

II Corinthians 6:18

When we consider the relationship we have with the Lord, it is all the more reason we should love and serve Him. "Behold, what manner of love the Father hath bestowed upon us, that we should be called the sons of God."

"And I will cleanse them from all their iniquity, whereby they have sinned against me; and I will pardon all their iniquities, whereby they have sinned, and whereby they have transgressed against me."

Jeremiah 33:8

If you have ever wondered how far the love of God would go, take another look at this. "I have loved thee with an everlasting love."

"He that covereth his sins shall not prosper: but whoso confesseth and forsaketh them shall have mercy."

Proverbs 28:13

The thing that may be holding us back is what we are hiding from God. Tell Him your problem. Whatever the problem, He is the answer. "If we confess our sins, he is faithful and just to forgive us our sins, and to cleanse us from all unrighteousness."

GOD'S LOVE

"Grace and peace be multiplied unto you through the knowledge of God, and of Jesus our Lord, According as his divine power hath given unto us all things that pertain unto life and godliness, through the knowledge of him that hath called us to glory and virtue."

II Peter 1:2,3

God has touched every base of human need to give us a full and beautiful life all the way home. How strange that we find it so hard to believe and receive. Believe what He says. Take what He offers. Thanks, Lord.

———————

Words of Guidance....

Words of Guidance

"And as ye would that men should do to you, do ye also to them likewise."

Luke 6:31

Here is the beginning of the new world you have always wanted to create.

"A man's pride shall bring him low: but honour shall uphold the humble in spirit."

Proverbs 29:23

Pride is a killer that has slain many spiritual giants. When a person gets wrapped up in himself, he makes a pretty small package.

"Holding forth the word of life; that I may rejoice in the day of Christ, that I have not run in vain, neither laboured in vain."

Philippians 2:16

Here's news, Christian friend. Our greatest job is not to explain the Word of God, but to extend it.

"Let the words of my mouth, and the meditation of my heart, be acceptable in thy sight, O Lord, my strength, and my redeemer."

Psalms 19:14

Not only what we talk about, but what we think about, is screened by the Lord. Is it acceptable to the Lord?

"Seest thou a man that is hasty in his words? there is more hope of a fool than of him."

Proverbs 29:20

Hasty words lead to rash decisions resulting so often in heartbreak. Think a little before you say a lot. Man shall "give an account of every idle word."

"Enter not into the path of the wicked, and go not in the way of evil men."

Proverbs 4:14

Don't ask for trouble by placing yourself in the path of the evildoer. We are in the world, but we don't have to be of it. Follow God's way as He says, "This is the way, walk ye in it."

". . . compel them to come in, that my house may be filled."

Luke 14:23

Put forth some effort for God. Recognize the urgency of the message that you have and find someone quick to tell it to. "Bring them in from the paths of sin." God's house is a hive for workers, not a rest for drones.

"Ye have lived in pleasure on the earth, and been wanton; ye have nourished your hearts, as in a day of slaughter."

James 5:5

Big times are not always good times. Only Jesus satisfies. "But seek ye first the kingdom of God, and his righteousness; and all these things shall be added unto you."

"Commit thy way unto the Lord; trust also in him; and he shall bring it to pass."

Psalms 37:5

The reason that the Lord doesn't bring a lot of things to pass is because He can't get past us. Move over and let God take the lead. "His ways are not our ways."

"And he gave them their request; but sent leanness into their soul."

Psalms 106:15

This is a high price to pay for determination to have your own way. Let God rule. He knows best.

"He that is slow to anger is better than the mighty; and he that ruleth his spirit than he that taketh a city."

Proverbs 16:32

To be strong at these points is to please God, to promote harmony, and to have peace. What more could we ask?

"Let your conversation be without covetousness; and be content with such things as ye have: for he hath said, I will never leave thee, nor forsake thee."

Hebrews 13:5

Use what you have while you live . . . for the glory of God and the good of mankind. This is the best way to keep it from having you.

――――――――

"If my people, which are called by my name, shall humble themselves, and pray, and seek my face, and turn from their wicked ways; then will I hear from heaven, and will forgive their sin, and will heal their land."

II Chronicles 7:14

God keeps coming back with the same prescription for recovery and we keep coming up with the same old postponement. "Seek ye first the kingdom of God, and his righteousness; and all these things shall be added unto you."

――――――――

"And he came to Nazareth, where he had been brought up: and, as his custom was, he went into the synagogue on the sabbath day, and stood up for to read.''

Luke 4:16

The next time you are inclined to think that the worship services at your church are not important, take another look at the Lord's practice. You need the church and the church needs you. ''Forsake not the assembling of yourselves together . . .''

———————

''And the Lord said unto me, Say unto them, Go not up, neither fight; for I am not among you; lest ye be smitten before your enemies.''

Deuteronomy 1:42

The person or nation that goes out to do battle with the forces of the world ought to be sure that they have the backing of Heaven. ''Without me, ye can do nothing.''

———————

''Lot . . . pitched his tent toward Sodom.''

Genesis 13:12

People who pitch their tent in the direction of evil ought not be surprised at the outcome after they have arrived.

———————

"But seek ye first the kingdom of God, and his righteousness; and all these things shall be added unto you."

Matthew 6:33

Our great problem has ever been to put material things in their right place. Let nothing keep you from your church and away from Christ.

———————

"No man can serve two masters: for either he will hate the one, and love the other; or else he will hold to the one, and despise the other. Ye cannot serve God and mammon."

Matthew 6:24

Man must make a clean break from the world if he is to have a close tie with Heaven.

———————

"As ye have therefore received Christ Jesus the Lord, so walk ye in him."

Colossians 2:6

It is as important to keep Him in our walk as it is to keep Him in our worship. A sermon in shoes stands out.

———————

"Bless them which persecute you: bless, and curse not."

Romans 12:14

There is no cure like kindness. Shock your enemy; return a little good for evil and you will be in for a surprise yourself.

———————

"For he that biddeth him God speed is partaker of his evil deeds."

II John 11

Many of us pat evil on the back by not saying a word. Silence can also be sinful.

———————

"There is a way which seemeth right unto a man, but the end thereof are the ways of death."

Proverbs 14:12

The unconverted man who follows his own conscience without conviction is on shaky ground. Let God guide you.

———————

"Commit thy way unto the Lord; trust also in him; and he shall bring it to pass."
Psalms 37:5

Our real strength lies in our whole-hearted surrender to His will and way. "Be strong in the Lord."

"Again, the kingdom of heaven is like unto a merchant man, seeking goodly pearls: Who, when he had found one pearl of great price, went and sold all that he had, and bought it."
Matthew 13:45,46

This is a lesson in majoring in main things. Put all that you have and all that you are in the one and only thing that really counts.

"Ye shall not make with me gods of silver, neither shall ye make unto you gods of gold."
Exodus 20:23

Gold makes a poor god and an overbearing master. "But seek ye first the kingdom of God, and his righteousness; and all these things shall be added unto you."

". . . whatsoever ye would that men should do to you, do ye even so to them . . ."

Matthew 7:12

Here are fifteen words that can change our lives.

"That ye might walk worthy of the Lord unto all pleasing, being fruitful in every good work, and increasing in the knowledge of God."

Colossians 1:10

We would really be doing something if our study and dedication to God's Word would keep step with our great search for education.

"If my people, which are called by my name, shall humble themselves, and pray, and seek my face, and turn from their wicked ways; then will I hear from heaven, and will forgive their sin, and will heal their land."

II Chronicles 7:14

Mr. Candidate, bring this great truth home to us as Americans, and God will honor you. Here is the platform that will never crumble. Take your stand here and take it to the American people. "Righteousness exalteth a nation: but sin is a reproach to any people."

———————

"The fear of the Lord is the beginning of knowledge: but fools despise wisdom and instruction."

Proverbs 1:7

This says something to the so-called intellectual who has completely ignored the main stream of real science and common sense and has branched off in pursuit of knowledge without God.

———————

"So Jotham became mighty, because he prepared his ways before the Lord his God."

II Chronicles 27:6

Power belongeth to God and is available to man. The man who does not take God into account in his preparation for life will have to reckon with Him as to why he didn't.

———————

"Judge not, and ye shall not be judged: condemn not, and ye shall not be condemned: forgive, and ye shall be forgiven."

Luke 6:37

Before we can be cleansed of our own faults, we must have everything in the clear with our neighbor. "If ye forgive not, neither will your heavenly Father forgive you."

———————

"Wisdom is the principal thing; therefore get wisdom: and with all thy getting get understanding."

Proverbs 4:7

We live in a world that has gone wild about everything but wisdom. Father God, give us wisdom, will power, and a desire that we have not as yet known to please You and win the world to Jesus. In His name and for Your glory. Amen.

———————

"Blessed is the man that walketh not in the counsel of the ungodly, nor standeth in the way of sinners, nor sitteth in the seat of the scornful."
Psalms 1:1

Find a man who is well disciplined at these three points and you will find a real disciple of God, though he may not say a word.

———————

"A man hath joy by the answer of his mouth: and a word spoken in due season, how good it is!"
Proverbs 15:23

The right word at the right time can really turn a situation around. Pray that it will come to you.

———————

"He that is slow to anger is better than the mighty; and he that ruleth his spirit than he that taketh a city."
Proverbs 16:32

The "in fighting" is what's rough. Win there and the victory is yours. Call up the inner man. "Greater is he that is in you, than he that is in the world."

———————

"The soul of the sluggard desireth, and hath nothing: but the soul of the diligent shall be made fat."

Proverbs 13:4

There is a lot to be said for doing, as well as dreaming. "Faith without works is dead." Work while it is day. The night cometh when no man can work.

"When a man's ways please the Lord, he maketh even his enemies to be at peace with him."

Proverbs 16:7

Here is another good reason for putting the Lord first. "Seek ye first the kingdom of God, and his righteousness; and all these things shall be added unto you."

"Good understanding giveth favour: but the way of transgressors is hard."

Proverbs 13:15

If for some reason you have gotten the idea that living the good life is hard, take another look at this truth. You will never re-live today. Make it a good one with God's help!

"O that ye would altogether hold your peace! and it should be your wisdom."

Job 13:5

Many times, saying nothing is about the smartest thing we can do.

"Looking diligently lest any man fail of the grace of God; lest any root of bitterness springing up trouble you, and thereby many be defiled."

Hebrews 12:15

We must fight negative thought patterns and poutings or else they will neutralize our lives, leaving us ineffective and miserable. Cheer up! God loves you and has plans for you beyond your greatest dreams.

"Then we which are alive and remain shall be caught up together with them in the clouds, to meet the Lord in the air: and so shall we ever be with the Lord."

I Thessalonians 4:17

Every Christian ought to be ready to go on a moment's notice and yet willing to work a lifetime waiting for His return. "Even so, come, Lord Jesus!"

"Let no man despise thy youth; but be thou an example of the believers, in word, in conversation, in charity, in spirit, in faith, in purity."
I Timothy 4:12

Life is a book of memories we start writing early to be read over and over again. Happy is the person who enjoys what he has written even when he is old.

―――――――

"Fret not thyself because of evildoers, neither be thou envious against the workers of iniquity."

Psalms 37:1

It is easy to get so wrapped up in condemning evil that we grow negligent in doing good.

―――――――

". . . when he shall come in his own glory, and in his Father's, and of the holy angels."
Luke 9:26

Don't think that you can ignore the Lord in this life and have Him make a lot over you in the life to come.

―――――――

". . . We will go with you: for we have heard that God is with you."

Zechariah 8:23

When you find a man who shows evidence of walking with the Lord, you will do well to join him. Make friends with those who are friends of God.

———————

"Let every man abide in the same calling wherein he was called."

I Corinthians 7:20

Every person has a place in life to fill and he has no peace until he finds it. Let God's will be your way.

———————

"But ye have set at nought all my counsel, and would none of my reproof."

Proverbs 1:25

The person traveling with a one-track mind is bound to have a head-on collision.

———————

"So teach us to number our days, that we may apply our hearts unto wisdom."

Psalms 90:12

Life is serious and should be lived seriously. That doesn't mean that all the pleasure is taken out of it. But it has a lot to do with cutting the mistakes to a minimum.

"Grudge not one against another, brethren, lest ye be condemned: behold, the judge standeth before the door."

James 5:9

Give up the grudge. It is not worth it. Too many victories have gone by the way already. "If you forgive not men their trespasses, neither will your Father forgive you."

"For he that soweth to his flesh shall of the flesh reap corruption; but he that soweth to the Spirit shall of the Spirit reap life everlasting."

Galatians 6:8

Life is a matter of sowing and reaping, and it is given to every man to determine the crop.

"Nay, in all these things we are more than conquerors through him that loved us."

Romans 8:37

Let us act like what God says we are, and watch despair disappear.

"Not forsaking the assembling of ourselves together, as the manner of some is; but exhorting one another: and so much the more, as ye see the day approaching."

Hebrews 10:25

If we could only see the value of obedience to God in this area, there would be such a run on the church that it would alarm the world and amaze the believer. Attend the Lord's house this week with your family. The rest of the week will go better at your house.

"And be ye kind one to another, tenderhearted, forgiving one another, even as God for Christ's sake hath forgiven you."

Ephesians 4:32

The life and example of Christ is not only to be admired, but followed.

"I exhort therefore, that, first of all, supplications, prayers, intercessions, and giving of thanks, be made for all men; For kings, and for all that are in authority; that we may lead a quiet and peaceable life in all godliness and honesty."

I Timothy 2:1,2

This is not a suggestion, but a directive. Let us obey. Father, we go beyond party lines as we put all elected officials on the prayer line. In this moment, we pray for our President and every other official, their families and the people they represent. Bless them with health, wisdom and spiritual perception through Jesus Christ our Lord. Amen.

———————

"Therefore I say unto you, Take no thought for your life, what ye shall eat, or what ye shall drink; nor yet for your body, what ye shall put on. Is not the life more than meat, and the body than raiment?"

Matthew 6:25

Here is where we put the most emphasis and Jesus said where we should put the least. "But seek ye first the kingdom of God, and his righteousness; and all these things shall be added unto you."

———————

"And as ye would that men should do to you, do ye also to them likewise."

Luke 6:31

Behold the great prescription of life! When properly administered and taken, it can clear up every disease of ill will known to man. We get the real picture of life as we major in the art of putting ourselves in each other's place.

———————

"Do this now, my son, and deliver thyself, when thou art come into the hand of thy friend; go, humble thyself, and make sure thy friend."

Proverbs 6:3

Take the humble position. The hardest things to do are very often the most rewarding.

———————

The Holy Spirit....

The Holy Spirit

"But when the Comforter is come, whom I will send unto you from the Father, even the Spirit of truth, which proceedeth from the Father, he shall testify of me."

John 15:26

The Holy Spirit is our constant companion and our Divine Teacher whose number one assignment is pointing us to Jesus. When we have learned that lesson, we will have pleased the Teacher, received power in our lives, and fulfilled the plan of the Father.

"But ye shall receive power, after that the Holy Ghost is come upon you: and ye shall be witnesses unto me both in Jerusalem, and in all Judea, and in Samaria, and unto the uttermost part of the earth."

Acts 1:8

Too long have we tried to produce on our own power and have discovered that we have the wrong connection and the lines were down. We must be filled with the Spirit or be content with human frustration.

"And he sent, and brought him in. Now he was ruddy, and withal of a beautiful countenance, and goodly to look to. And the Lord said, Arise, anoint him: for this is he. Then Samuel took the horn of oil, and anointed him in the midst of his brethren: and the Spirit of the Lord came upon David from that day forward."

I Samuel 16:12,13

The Spirit of the Lord upon a man is still the best credential that he can have . . . and probably the only one that God recognizes.

"And the Lord shall guide thee continually, and satisfy thy soul in drought, and make fat thy bones: and thou shalt be like a watered garden, and like a spring of water, whose waters fail not."

Isaiah 58:11

God guides us through the inspiration of His Word, the inner impression of His presence and through circumstances that He has created or allowed. The Holy Spirit will guide you into all truth. Let Him!

"If ye then, being evil, know how to give good gifts unto your children: how much more shall your heavenly Father give the Holy Spirit to them that ask him?''

Luke 11:13

With the thought in mind that God is surely as concerned and capable as you are in also giving you His best, simply open your heart and receive. "No good thing will he withhold from them that walk uprightly."

"And I knew him not: but he that sent me to baptize with water, the same said unto me, Upon whom thou shalt see the Spirit descending, and remaining on him, the same is he which baptizeth with the Holy Ghost."

John 1:33

There is no spiritual experience outside of the Saviour.

"And the spirit entered into me when he spake unto me, and set me upon my feet, that I heard him that spake unto me."

Ezekiel 2:2

When the Spirit of God enters the human life, It becomes the vessel through which God speaks and lives are touched.

"But ye shall receive power, after that the Holy Ghost is come upon you: and ye shall be witnesses unto me both in Jerusalem, and in all Judea, and in Samaria, and unto the uttermost part of the earth."

Acts 1:8

It's God's Holy Spirit that gives us something to say and the power to go with it. How futile to keep struggling in the flesh. Holy Spirit, fill us with Your presence and send us out with Your power in the service of God, in Jesus name. Amen.

"Likewise the Spirit also helpeth our infirmities: for we know not what we should pray for as we ought: but the Spirit itself maketh intercession for us with groanings which cannot be uttered. And he that searcheth the hearts knoweth what is the mind of the Spirit, because he maketh intercession for the saints according to the will of God."

Romans 8:26,27

Invite the Holy Spirit to intercede for you and through you. You will discover it is a passing gear and an overdrive in your prayer life far beyond what you ever dreamed possible.

"Then he answered and spake unto me, saying, This is the word of the Lord unto Zerubbabel, saying, Not by might, nor by power, but by my spirit, saith the Lord of hosts."

Zechariah 4:6

Simply turn it over to the Holy Spirit. He takes the strain and suspense out of it all. Oh Holy Spirit, in Jesus' name and for the glory of God, move in and through us and do what Jesus would be doing if He were here in person. In His name, Amen.

"And it shall come to pass afterward, that I will pour out my spirit upon all flesh; and your sons and your daughters shall prophesy, your old men shall dream dreams, your young men shall see visions: And also upon the servants and upon the handmaids in those days will I pour out my spirit."

Joel 2:28,29

We can see the evidence of that day in our time and, though many cannot understand it, none of us can deny it. Holy Spirit, breathe on us and empower us to evangelize the world in our time. In Jesus' name, Amen.

———————

". . . Not by might, nor by power, but by my spirit, saith the Lord of Hosts."

Zechariah 4:6

We are guilty of depending on our own working and wisdom, and not depending upon the Holy Spirit and His power. If we would be happy in our Christian experience, we need to relieve ourselves of the strain of so many works of our own and submit all to the guidance of the Holy Spirit.

———————

''And the Spirit of the Lord began to move him at times . . .''

Judges 13:25

Don't be satisfied with an occasional moving of the Spirit when we can have showers of blessing all the time. The anointing of the Spirit requires an ignoring of self.

''Then he answered and spake unto me, saying, This is the word of the Lord unto Zerubbabel, saying, Not by might, nor by power, but by my spirit, saith the Lord of hosts.''

Zechariah 4:6

No program, project or person can ever take the place of the Holy Spirit. The sooner the Church replaces the strain of pushing with the Spirit's leading, the easier our task will be.

''And, behold, I send the promise of my Father upon you: but tarry ye in the city of Jerusalem, until ye be endued with power from on high.''

Luke 24:49

The Lord never meant for us to work for Him under our own power. Our lack of success can probably be traced to the fact that we leaned on self and ignored the Spirit.

"Quench not the Spirit."

I Thessalonians 5:19

There is no substitute for the Spirit of God. "If any man have not the Spirit of God, he is none of his."

"The Holy Ghost shall teach you in the same hour what ye ought to say."

Luke 12:12

Rely on the Holy Spirit. He has both the answer and the authority of the Father. "Greater is he that is in you than he that is in the world."

"And he said, My presence shall go with thee, and I will give thee rest."

Exodus 33:14

The Lord's power, pardon and presence is available.

"Ye stiffnecked and uncircumcised in heart and ears, ye do always resist the Holy Ghost: as your fathers did, so do ye."

Acts 7:51

This is part of a sermon that needs repeating often. It is a dangerous thing to resist the Holy Spirit. "My spirit shall not always strive with man." "Today if ye will hear his voice, harden not your heart."

"But the fruit of the Spirit is love, joy, peace, longsuffering, gentleness, goodness, faith, Meekness, temperance: against such there is no law."

Galatians 5:22,23

Here are the fruits of the Spirit, the outgrowth of the indwelling of His great presence. "By this shall all men know that ye are my disciples, if ye have love one to another."

"Now we have received, not the spirit of the world, but the spirit which is of God; that we might know the things that are freely given to us of God."

I Corinthians 2:12

Thank God for all the promises we have in Him. Jesus made them all possible. The Spirit of God makes them all known.

"For to one is given by the Spirit the word of wisdom; to another the word of knowledge by the same Spirit; . . . To another the working of miracles; to another prophecy; to another discerning of spirits; to another divers kinds of tongues; to another the interpretation of tongues."

I Corinthians 12:8,10

Here are the gifts of the Spirit, given to be shared as starters for all else that God has for those who open up themselves to be used of Him.

"Likewise the Spirit also helpeth our infirmities: for we know not what we should pray for as we ought: but the Spirit itself maketh intercession for us with groanings which cannot be uttered."

Romans 8:26

When we pray in the Spirit, we get to the heart of the matter! Holy Spirit, take our thoughts and our tongues and pray through us that we may touch God with our real need in Jesus' name, Amen.

"But the anointing which ye have received of him abideth in you, and ye need not that any man teach you: but as the same anointing teacheth you of all things, and is truth, and is no lie, and even as it hath taught you, ye shall abide in him."

I John 2:27

Stop looking at what is going on around you and draw upon the strength of His Spirit who lives within you. "Greater is he that is in you than he that is in the world."

"But if the Spirit of him that raised up Jesus from the dead dwell in you, he that raised up Christ from the dead shall also quicken your mortal bodies by his Spirit that dwelleth in you."

Romans 8:11

Look at the power of the Holy Spirit! And if you are a Christian, He is in you to bring to pass all the powerful things that God meant for you to have.

Jesus, Lord and Saviour....

Jesus, Lord and Saviour

". . . This is my beloved Son, in whom I am well pleased."

Matthew 3:17

Jesus came into the world, lived under great hardships and died on the cross to satisfy His Father. What have you done to please Him?

"But a certain Samaritan, as he journeyed, came where he was: and when he saw him, he had compassion on him, And went to him, and bound up his wounds, pouring in oil and wine, and set him on his own beast, and brought him to an inn, and took care of him."

Luke 10:33,34

This is like Jesus. He always comes to where we are with all that we need and just in time. Don't worry about the ones who have passed you by. Think about the One who has gone all the way for you.

"Jesus saith unto him, I am the way, the truth, and the life: no man cometh unto the Father, but by me."

John 14:6

Jesus is the way to eternal life and any detour that we make for ourselves will only lead to a dead end. Ask Him boldly now to bless you with His presence and He will. "Behold, I stand at the door and knock: if any man will open the door, I will come in."

". . . Never man spake like this man."

John 7:46

No one ever talked like Jesus; no one ever walked like Jesus; no one ever cared like Jesus.

"This Jesus hath God raised up, whereof we all are witnesses."

Acts 2:32

Death, man's most dreaded enemy, has become a servant instead of a slave master, all because of the love of God and the sacrifice of His Son. "Oh death, where is thy sting?" "Because I live, ye shall live also."

". . . What manner of man is this, that even the wind and the sea obey him?"

Mark 4:41

Man can report the weather, but only God can do anything about it. Turn your storm-tossed life over to the One who will banish every fear. "Fear not, I am with thee."

―――――――――

"And the men that held Jesus mocked him, and smote him."

Luke 22:63

Today, Jesus is mocked and crucified anew by unbelief and indifference by a self-sufficient world and a lukewarm Church.

―――――――――

"Jesus said unto her, I am the resurrection, and the life: he that believeth in me, though he were dead, yet shall he live."

John 11:25

Jesus conquered death and claims the same victory for all who confess Him as Saviour. "O death, where is thy sting? O grave, where is thy victory?"

―――――――――

"But God commendeth his love toward us, in that, while we were yet sinners, Christ died for us."

Romans 5:8

The Lord takes us as we are to make us what we ought to be and what we really want to be. Christ is not only the answer, but the difference.

———————

"Jesus Christ the same yesterday, and to day, and for ever."

Hebrews 13:8

Once a person really believes that Christ is the same, he himself will never be the same.

———————

"If we suffer, we shall also reign with him: if we deny him, he also will deny us."

II Timothy 2:12

Don't put the Lord in the background here and expect Him to make a fuss over you in Heaven. The Saviour that you deny here will be the Saviour that you will meet in eternity.

———————

"But God forbid that I should glory, save in the cross of our Lord Jesus Christ . . ."

Galatians 6:14

The cross is a constant reminder that we are helpless in the saving of our own soul. It was Christ who died and rose again to put eternal hope within reach of all.

". . . his name shall be called Wonderful, Counseller, The mighty God, The everlasting Father, The Prince of Peace."

Isaiah 9:6

He has been true to His name and true to His Word. He is qualified to help you in every area of life. Trust Him today!

"Who his own self bare our sins in his own body on the tree . . ."

I Peter 2:24

The sins of the whole world were borne by the Saviour, but every person must come individually to the cross to secure the pardon. He will set you free.

"I am that bread of life."

John 6:48

Only the Saviour can fully satisfy the longing soul and the burdened heart. He still feeds the hungry multitudes in life's wilderness.

"I am he that liveth, and was dead; and, behold, I am alive for evermore, Amen; and have the keys of hell and of death."

Revelation 1:18

The living Christ is at the right hand of the living God, ready to save a world dead in trespasses and sins.

"The thief cometh not, but for to steal, and to kill, and to destroy: I am come that they might have life, and that they might have it more abundantly."

John 10:10

God is for us having the good things of life. This is why Jesus came. Why settle for less?

"And from Jesus Christ, who is the faithful witness, and the first begotten of the dead, and the prince of the kings of the earth. Unto him that loved us, and washed us from our sins in his own blood, And hath made us kings and priests unto God and his Father; to him be glory and dominion for ever and ever. Amen."

Revelation 1:5,6

There was only one way to deal with the sin problem, and Jesus became the answer. Turn it all over to Him. The cleansing is complete and it is free. He is faithful and just to cleanse us from all sin.

———————

"But God commendeth his love toward us, in that, while we were yet sinners, Christ died for us. Much more then, being now justified by his blood, we shall be saved from wrath through him."

Romans 5:8,9

The death of Jesus could not wait on our decision. He died in advance of what we would do. Even at this late date, "What will you do with Jesus?"

———————

"In the last day, that great day of the feast, Jesus stood and cried, saying, If any man thirst, let him come unto me, and drink."

John 7:37

Here is the real thirst slaker. If you are weary of the desert and tired of the search, turn to the Divine Saviour who will meet your need and forgive your sins.

———————

"And always, night and day, he was in the mountains, and in the tombs, crying, and cutting himself with stones. But when he saw Jesus afar off, he ran and worshipped him."

Mark 5:5,6

Here is the story of a man who got tired of living in the scary surroundings of the tombs and came to the Saviour for relief. Are you living on an island in the tombs of fear and doubt? There is more to life than that. Jesus is coming your way. Receive Him.

———————

"Now when he was in Jerusalem at the passover, in the feast day, many believed in his name, when they saw the miracles which he did."

John 2:23

He was a miracle worker then. He is a miracle worker forever. "Jesus Christ the same yesterday, and today and forever."

———————

"He that believeth on him is not condemned: but he that believeth not is condemned already, because he hath not believed in the name of the only begotten Son of God."

John 3:18

The unbeliever's future is already settled. Only an act of faith in the acceptance of Jesus Christ can regenerate him and reverse his destiny.

———————

"Jesus answered and said unto him, What I do thou knowest not now; but thou shalt know hereafter."

John 13:7

It's not all that important that we know all that He does, so long as we are sure we know Him.

———————

"But as many as received him, to them gave he power to become the sons of God, even to them that believe on his name."

John 1:12

Our right relation with God is contingent upon what we do with His Son.

———————

"And lo a voice from heaven, saying, This is my beloved Son, in whom I am well pleased."
Matthew 3:17

It seems so incredible that so much of earth should ignore what all of Heaven has endorsed. "God so loved the world that he gave his Son . . ."

———————

"But as many as received him, to them gave he power to become the sons of God, even to them that believe on his name."

John 1:12

A strained relationship between you and the Saviour is a sure separator between you and God. Jesus said, "No man cometh unto the Father, but by me."

———————

"Who his own self bare our sins in his own body on the tree, that we, being dead to sins, should live unto righteousness: by whose stripes ye were healed."

I Peter 2:24

The death of Jesus Christ upon the cross carried with it an atonement for soul and body. The sad report of so many of us is that we are reluctant to trust Him for either.

———————

"And she shall bring forth a son, and thou shalt call his name JESUS: for he shall save his people from their sins."

Matthew 1:21

The whole world can sympathize, but only Jesus can save. Jesus saves, keeps and satisfies.

———————

"The thief cometh not, but for to steal, and to kill, and to destroy: I am come that they might have life, and that they might have it more abundantly."

John 10:10

Life really begins at the age when the "Rock of Ages" takes over. Contrary to what you may think, the Lord is in favor of you having more of life, not less, and more reason to live it. You can live it up all the way to Heaven.

"And being found in fashion as a man, he humbled himself, and became obedient unto death, even the death of the cross."

Philippians 2:8

We must never forget that it took Christ going to the cross to cancel out our sins. It is not until we come to Him that we become a part of what He has provided.

"In whom we have redemption through his blood, even the forgiveness of sins."

Colossians 1:14

In Jesus we have redemption, release, reward, and the revelation of the Father. It's all in Him and, without Him, all is in vain.

"But as many as received him, to them gave he power to become the sons of God, even to them that believe on his name."

John 1:12

We become a part of the family of God based on our relations with His Son.

———————

"But thanks be to God, which giveth us the victory through our Lord Jesus Christ."

I Corinthians 15:57

Too much time is spent in planning battles and fighting wars that have already been won. Take what He gives and give what He asks.

———————

"Jesus, when he had cried again with a loud voice, yielded up the ghost."

Matthew 27:50

We must never forget that Calvary was full of pain as well as pardon. "Christ suffered for us."

———————

"I am that bread of life. Your fathers did eat manna in the wilderness, and are dead. This is the bread which cometh down from heaven, that a man may eat thereof, and not die.''

John 6:48-50

There is no hunger like soul hunger, and there is nothing that will satisfy it but the Saviour. "Come and dine, the Master calleth . . come and dine.''

''But this cometh to pass, that the word might be fulfilled that is written in their law, They hated me without a cause.''

John 15:25

Don't be so hard on people who rejected the Saviour in the past. If up to this point you have not accepted Him, you are in the same company. Why have you rejected Him? Right now, ask Him to come into your heart and He will.

"For other foundation can no man lay than that is laid, which is Jesus Christ."

I Corinthians 3:11

Nothing can be added to what our Divine Advocate did. To mix anything man-made as a means of our Salvation is to insult God and sink all hopes of our eternal life with Him.

"And when he was accused of the chief priests and elders, he answered nothing."

Matthew 27:12

The answer of Jesus was in His submission to the crucifixtion for the sins of all. By His death and resurrection, He is still speaking to all who are bound in sin and seeking to go free.

"And they spit upon him, and took the reed, and smote him on the head. And after that they had mocked him, they took the robe off from him, and put his own raiment on him, and led him away to crucify him."

Matthew 27:30,31

While it may seem unbelievable that it could happen, it is equally unbelievable that so many could forget it! "Christ died for our sins."

———————

"Jesus said unto her, I am the resurrection, and the life: he that believeth in me, though he were dead, yet shall he live."

John 11:25

Keep remembering that He is the giver of life and the master of death. "Because I live, ye shall live also."

———————

"And daily in the temple, and in every house, they ceased not to teach and preach Jesus Christ."

Acts 5:42

He was all of it! If we are to experience what they enjoyed, the emphasis must again be placed upon Jesus. "Neither is there salvation in any other: for there is none other name under heaven given among men, whereby we must be saved."

———————

"And he saith unto them, Why are ye fearful, O ye of little faith? Then he arose, and rebuked the winds and the sea; and there was a great calm."

Matthew 8:26

No man can afford to face the storms of life without the Divine Captain. His presence alone brings calmness, confidence, and courage.

"For had ye believed Moses, ye would have believed me: for he wrote of me."

John 5:46

The whole world of God revolves around His Son, our Saviour. Our whole destiny depends on what we believe about it and what we do about it. "If ye believe not that I am he, ye shall die in your sins."

"Jesus saith unto him, I am the way, the truth, and the life: no man cometh unto the Father, but by me."

John 14:6

Jesus is not a way among many ways, but THE way. How foolish to look for detours.

"Jesus saith unto her, Woman, why weepest thou? whom seekest thou?"

John 20:15

The only One who can heal the broken heart is interested in every tear and every trial. "He careth for you."

"He maketh me to lie down in green pastures: he leadeth me beside the still waters."

Psalms 23:2

Only the Saviour can take the strain out of life . . . and the fear out of death.

"Now unto him that is able to keep you from falling, and to present you faultless before the presence of his glory with exceeding joy."

Jude 24

He is not only a Saviour, but a keeper. "Praise ye the Lord."

"But as many as received him, to them gave he power to become the sons of God, even to them that believe on his name."

John 1:12

Our right relation with God is contingent upon what we do with His Son.

"Jesus saith unto him, I am the way, the truth, and the life: no man cometh unto the Father, but by me."

John 14:6

No man ignores the Son and reaches the Father. "He that believeth not the Son shall not see life; but the wrath of God abideth on him."

"Come, see a man, which told me all things that ever I did: is not this the Christ?"

John 4:29

It is a sobering thing to know that the One you may be rejecting knows you so well and holds the power of life and death over you.

"And she brought forth her firstborn son . . . and laid him in a manger; because there was no room for them in the inn."

Luke 2:7

Our lives are like inns along the road of life, and Jesus is still at the door, waiting to come in and occupy His rightful place. Make room for Him.

"Thomas saith unto him, Lord, we know not whither thou goest; and how can we know the way?"

John 14:5

Jesus saith unto him, "I am the way, the truth, and the life: no man cometh to the Father, but by me."

"And Mary said, My soul doth magnify the Lord."

Luke 1:46

How wonderful it would be if we stopped magnifying the church, creeds and the credentials of man, and simply magnified Jesus Christ.

"Seeing then that we have a great high priest, that is passed into the heavens, Jesus the Son of God, let us hold fast our profession."

Hebrews 4:14

There is nothing on the earth that our Saviour in Heaven can't handle. He ever liveth to make intercession for us.

"To whom also he shewed himself alive after his passion by many infallible proofs, being seen of them forty days, and speaking of the things pertaining to the kingdom of God."

Acts 1:3

It is a matter of record that He lived, died, and rose again. He now lives at the right hand of the Father and in the hearts of believers. "He is risen, as he said."

"For unto us a child is born, unto us a son is given: and the government shall be upon his shoulder: and his name shall be called Wonderful, Counsellor, The mighty God, The everlasting Father, The Prince of Peace."

Isaiah 9:6

The world would breathe easier if God had more of a part in the governments today, and as for that matter, if He had more of a prominent part in our churches.

"Beware lest any man spoil you through philosophy and vain deceit, after the tradition of men, after the rudiments of the world, and not after Christ."

Colossians 2:8

If what you know or hear in the name of Christianity does not exalt Christ and glorify God, put it down as man made and not Heaven sent. The Holy Spirit is our ally of discernment and will direct us.

"Who is he that condemneth? It is Christ that died, yea rather, that is risen again, who is even at the right hand of God, who also maketh intercession for us."

Romans 8:34

We need to keep remembering that it was Jesus who died for our sins, and that He is alive, forevermore interceding for us.

"And whatsoever ye do in word or deed, do all in the name of the Lord Jesus, giving thanks to God and the Father by him."

Colossians 3:17

If we want to make what we do count, it must be done in Christ's name and for His cause and with thanks.

———————

"In whom we have redemption through his blood, even the forgiveness of sins."

Colossians 1:14

Nothing less and nothing more can settle the sin question in our lives. The blood of Jesus Christ, God's Son, cleanseth us from all sins. The application is in acknowledging that He died for us and we cannot really live without Him.

———————

Love....

Love

"And I will very glady spend and be spent for you; though the more abundantly I love you, the less I be loved."

II Corinthians 12:15

This is the only language that a confused world understands. A love that is not only vocal, but active. It is not what we say, but what we do that counts.

"He therefore that despiseth, despiseth not man, but God, who hath also given unto us his holy Spirit."

I Thessalonians 4:8

Our attitude toward our earthly brother is a good indication how we actually feel toward our Heavenly Father. "Love one another."

". . . to love his neighbour as himself, is more than all whole burnt offerings and sacrifices."

Mark 12:33

It's not what we offer up, but what we think of our fellow man that impresses God. Money without mercy is meaningless.

"And this commandment have we from him, That he who loveth God love his brother also."

I John 4:21

God accepts no love that includes Him and excludes our fellow man. This is the identifying mark of a Christian. Does the world recognize you as such?

"For the love of Christ constraineth us . . ."

II Corinthians 5:14

Self gives way to the Saviour when the love of Christ gets control of the heart. What the world needs today is more compassion and less censure.

"Charity suffereth long, and is kind; charity envieth not; charity vaunteth not itself, is not puffed up."

I Corinthians 13:4

Here is a test of true love. It's not all of it, but enough to let us know if we have the real thing.

"And Ruth said, Intreat me not to leave thee, or to return from following after thee: for whither thou goest, I will go; and where thou lodgest, I will lodge: thy people shall be my people, and thy God my God."

Ruth 1:16

Love is a mysterious force imparted by God the Father and gloriously shared by His creatures to degrees beyond human comprehension and reason. No wonder the Lord said of the first Christians, "By this shall all men know that ye are my disciples, if ye have love one to another."

———————

"But I say unto you, Love your enemies, bless them that curse you, do good to them that hate you, and pray for them which despitefully use you, and persecute you."

Matthew 5:44

If the spirit of Christ surfaces at this point in your life, you will know that you have done more than joined a church. All men will know that "Ye are my disciples, if ye have love one to another."

———————

"Master, which is the great commandment in the law? Jesus said unto him, Thou shalt love

the Lord thy God with all thy heart, and with all thy soul, and with all thy mind. This is the first and great commandment. And the second is like unto it, Thou shalt love thy neighbour as thyself.''
Matthew 22:36-39

The reason the world is in trouble to-day is because we have made so little over the great commandment. "Love covers a multitude of sins."

––––––––––

''But as touching brotherly love ye need not that I write unto you: for ye yourselves are taught of God to love one another.''
I Thessalonians 4:9

It is not religious talk, but the love of God relived in Christian acts of the believer that will win this world to Jesus. "In word and deed . . .''

––––––––––

"Now when they saw the boldness of Peter and John, and perceived that they were unlearned and ignorant men, they marvelled; and they took knowledge of them, that they had been with Jesus."

Acts 4:13

Do something Christ-like! Love people. It is not only have we told someone about Jesus, but have we shown them.

"A friend loveth at all times, and a brother is born for adversity."

Proverbs 17:17

There ought to be a day set aside as "good friend day", and they should be told so. Today would be a good day to say it. "What a friend we have in Jesus." Start with Him. He is a friend that sticketh closer than a brother. Tell Him and others how much you love and appreciate them. "A friend loveth at all times."

"That they all may be one; as thou, Father, art in me, and I in thee, that they also may be one in us: that the world may believe that thou hast sent me."

John 17:21

This is a portion of the prayer of Jesus. Everyone of us should do our part in bringing it to pass. He said, "Love one another as I have loved you."

"And the multitude of them that believed were of one heart and of one soul: neither said any of them that ought of the things which he possessed was his own; but they had all things common."

Acts 4:32

Genuine Christianity always makes its appearance in the form of great love and compassion for others. "The greatest of these is love."

"And though I bestow all my goods to feed the poor, and though I give my body to be burned, and have not charity, it profiteth me nothing."
I Corinthians 13:3

God sees the heart behind the hand and the motive behind the gift.

"I am that bread of life."

John 6:48

In an age of miracles and mechanism, it is a sad report that half of the world goes to bed with empty stomachs because the other half retires with empty hearts.

––––––––––

"And this is love, that we walk after his commandments . . ."

II John 6

A shallow Christian will walk after his own desires, but love will prompt a person to "walk after his commandments." Follow the leader and always make sure that the leader is Christ.

––––––––––

"We know that we have passed from death unto life, because we love the brethren. He that loveth not his brother abideth in death."

I John 3:14

One of the big signs of the new birth is how we feel about other believers in Christ, irregardless of their church.

––––––––––

"Thou shalt not avenge, nor bear any grudge against the children of thy people, but thou shalt love thy neighbour as thyself: I am the Lord."
Leviticus 19:18

Lack of love has been the undoing of humanity.

"For God so loved the world, that he gave his only begotten Son, that whosoever believeth in him should not perish, but have everlasting life."
John 3:16

God's love is big enough to cover the world and, yet, individual enough so that the least of us are included.

"This is my commandment, That ye love one another, as I have loved you."
John 15:12

All the world's problems through Jesus will be settled at this point or not at all. "Now abideth faith, hope, love; the greatest of these is love."

"But God commendeth his love toward us, in that, while we were yet sinners, Christ died for us."

Romans 5:8

It is not until we see ourselves as sinners that we can get a glimpse of the love of God, who sent Christ to die for the best and the worst of us. "Herein is love, not that we loved God, but that he loved us, and sent his Son . . ."

"I will love thee, O Lord, my strength."
Psalms 18:1

If the love of God is in our hearts, we will show it in our lives. "By this shall all men know that ye are my disciples, if ye have love one to another."

"Hatred stirreth up strifes: but love covereth all sins."

Proverbs 10:12

The degree of our love for God is reflected in our willingness to forgive our fellow man. Love covers a lot of sin and reflects a great deal more spirit.

"And why beholdest thou the mote that is in thy brother's eye, but considerest not the beam that is in thine own eye?"

Matthew 7:3

Our vision always seems at its best when we are looking at another's faults. Oh God, give us good "insight" so that we can be understanding of others. In Jesus' name. Amen.

———————

"For where envying and strife is, there is confusion and every evil work."

James 3:16

It is so true. These two things open the door to a runaway of everything that is ungodly and unwholesome for a life or a nation. Only God can close the door and bring harmony and peace. "Love one another."

———————

"For if ye love them which love you, what reward have ye? do not even the publicans the same?"

Matthew 5:46

True Christianity makes a difference and will be demonstrated in "down to earth" works and "Christ-like" love.

"We know that we have passed from death unto life, because we love the brethren. He that loveth not his brother abideth in death."

I John 3:14

Behold the evidence of the changed life. Say it with love. "By this shall all men know that ye are my disciples . . ."

"And now abideth faith, hope, charity, these three; but the greatest of these is charity."

I Corinthians 13:13

Love is the greatest force on earth and the prescription for the good life. Why don't we take it in and give it out?

Obedience to God....

Obedience to God

"Let the words of my mouth, and the meditation of my heart, be acceptable in thy sight, O Lord, my strength, and my redeemer."

Psalms 19:14

Not only what we talk about, but what we think about is screened by the Lord. Is it acceptable to the Lord?

"It repenteth me that I have set up Saul to be king: for he is turned back from following me, and hath not performed my commandments. And it grieved Samuel; and he cried unto the Lord all night."

I Samuel 15:11

Saul's problem is a common one. He thought his "over all performance" was good enough to see him through. All the while, God was placing the emphasis on obedience to specific directives. God has not changed. "Obedience is better than sacrifice."

"I am the God of Bethel, where thou anointedst the pillar, and where thou vowedst a vow unto me: now arise, get thee out from this land, and return unto the land of thy kindred."

Genesis 31:13

God has a running account of our kept and forgotten vows, and so often as the occasion arises, He calls for their fulfillment.

———————————

"And the Lord said unto me, Arise, get thee down quickly from hence; for thy people which thou hast brought forth out of Egypt have corrupted themselves; they are quickly turned aside out of the way which I commanded them; they have made them a molten image."

Deuteronomy 9:12

Humanity has not changed. When we lose touch with the true and living God, we start making our own. "Thou shalt worship the Lord thy God, and him only shalt thou serve."

———————————

"Howbeit when he, the Spirit of truth, is come, he will guide you into all truth: for he shall not speak of himself; but whatsoever he shall hear, that shall he speak: and he will shew you things to come."

John 16:13

One of our great problems is that we ask God for answers and guidance and then debate Him over His response. "Whatsoever he saith to you, do it." "We ought to obey God."

"Whether therefore ye eat, or drink, or whatsoever ye do, do all to the glory of God."
I Corinthians 10:31

Here is the argument settler. If you can't do a thing in accordance with His Word and will, don't do it. "Not my will, but thine, be done."

". . . All that the Lord hath said will we do, and be obedient."

Exodus 24:7

God's paths are clear. It is our dull hearing that gets us into trouble. "Obedience is better than sacrifice." "We ought to obey God rather than man."

"But this thing commanded I them, saying, Obey my voice, and I will be your God, and ye shall be my people: and walk ye in all the ways that I have commanded you, that it may be well unto you."

Jeremiah 7:23

Here is a condition and a promise that we cannot afford to ignore if we are to live happy and fruitful lives.

"And Jesus said unto them, Come ye after me, and I will make you to become fishers of men."

Mark 1:17

Jesus beckons us to the world's greatest business. Only in eternity will we see just how great. Stop what you are doing and follow Jesus in this, the most rewarding work of all! "He that winneth souls is wise."

"His lord said unto him, Well done, thou good and faithful servant: thou hast been faithful over a few things, I will make thee ruler over many things: enter thou into the joy of thy lord."

Matthew 25:21

Contrary to what we sometimes think, we will be rewarded not for our success but on the basis of our faithfulness. "Be thou faithful unto death, and I will give thee a crown of life."

"Then the king commanded, and they brought Daniel, and cast him into the den of lions. Now the king spake and said unto Daniel, Thy God whom thou servest continually, he will deliver thee."

Daniel 6:16

Our job is dedication - His is deliverance. If we give attention to doing His will, the Lord is good enough to give us even beyond what we ask.

"If they obey and serve him, they shall spend their days in prosperity, and their years in pleasures."

Job 36:11

Behold the emphasis on obedience and service! Looking for a success formula? Who can afford to overlook this one? Whatever the problem, He is the answer. Obey and follow Him.

"The Lord is my shepherd: I shall not want."

Psalms 23:1

The responsibiity of caring for and leading belongs to the shepherd; the responsibility of obedience and following belongs to the sheep.

"And hereby we do know that we know him, if we keep his commandments."

I John 2:3

The person who is well acquainted with the Lord will not be a stranger to His commandments.

"For your obedience is come abroad unto all men. I am glad therefore on your behalf . . ."
Romans 16:19

Men who listen to what God has to say will usually have an audience to hear what they have to say. "Obedience is better than sacrifice."

"If my people, which are called by my name, shall humble themselves, and pray, and seek my face, and turn from their wicked ways; then will I hear from heaven, and will forgive their sin, and will heal their land."
II Chronicles 7:14

The crisis will pass when we meet God's conditions. "Call upon me in the day of trouble: I will deliver thee, and thou shalt glorify me."

"And he did that which was right in the sight of the Lord . . ."
II Kings 15:34

If we major in what is right in God's sight, we don't have to worry about what it will look like in the eyes of man.

"And the disciples went, and did as Jesus commmanded them."

Matthew 21:6

The greatest need of the Church today is wholehearted obedience and down to earth preaching. "As my Father hath sent me, even so send I you."

"Teach me to do thy will . . ."

Psalms 143:10

The will of God will almost invariably be contrary to the ways of man. "For my thoughts are not your thoughts, neither are your ways my ways, saith the Lord."

"Blessed are they that do his commandments, that they may have right to the tree of life, and may enter in through the gates into the city."

Revelation 22:14

No man owns a part of that city until God owns all of that man.

"My sheep hear my voice, and I know them, and they follow me."

John 10:27

Father, we know that if You are mighty to save, then You can surely speak to us. Give us Your Divine directions today by Your spoken Word, and may we have obedience to follow, in Jesus' name. Amen.

"And thou shalt love the Lord thy God with all thine heart, and with all thy soul, and with all thy might '

Deuteronomy 6:5

God is not looking for a few shares in our life, but controlling interest. Nothing else will please Him—or us.

"No man can serve two masters: for either he will hate the one, and love the other; or else he will hold to the one, and despise the other. Ye cannot serve God and mammon."

Matthew 6:24

It takes a sell-out to do business with God. "Thou shalt have no other gods before me."

Our Every Need....

Our Every Need

"Cast not away therefore your confidence, which hath great recompence of reward."
Hebrews 10:35

If you are hanging out there on a low limb, don't forget the One who made the tree. Look up, the Lord is waiting to give you a hand . . . and a new heart. Father, touch the ones who are struggling just now, and give them strength, in Jesus' name. Amen.

"As soon as Jesus heard the word that was spoken, he saith unto the ruler of the synagogue, Be not afraid, only believe."
Mark 5:36

Fear not! Right now, if you invite Christ to take over your crisis, immediately you have all the power of Heaven in back of you. After the crisis, don't forget Him.

"Again I say unto you, That if two of you shall agree on earth as touching any thing that they shall ask, it shall be done for them of my Father which is in heaven."
Matthew 18:19

How simple! How Scriptural! Let's try it. Let's believe it. Think of a need that must be met. Whatever it may be, I will agree with you that it will be met now. In the name of Jesus and for the glory of God. Amen.

"The Lord executeth righteousness and judgment for all that are oppressed."

Psalms 103:6

Don't ever feel that the Lord is unaware of your burden. "He knoweth our frames." He knows the capacity of the load that we can carry and is standing by to shoulder it with us. "My help cometh from the Lord."

"And there sat a certain man at Lystra, impotent in his feet, being a cripple from his mother's womb, who never had walked: The same heard Paul speak: who steadfastly beholding him, and perceiving that he had faith to be healed, Said with a loud voice, Stand upright on thy feet. And he leaped and walked."

Acts 14:8-10

As long as there are men with needs, there will be a God of miracles to meet them. "I am the Lord thy God, I change not." "Jesus Christ, the same yesterday, and today, and for ever."

"Hitherto have ye asked nothing in my name: ask, and ye shall receive, that your joy may be full."

John 16:24

Don't think you can ever overdraw the account of your Heavenly Father. He . . . "will supply all your need according to his riches in glory by Christ Jesus."

". . . I am the Lord that healeth thee."
Exodus 15:26

The healing from God covers the whole range of man from his soul and mind to his body . . . even to his material need! "God is no respector of persons." Whatever He has done for others, He can do it again for you. "I am the Lord, I change not." Holy Spirit, touch the need of this reader in the name of Jesus and for the glory of God. Amen.

"And we know that all things work together for good to them that love God, to them who are the called according to his purpose."
Romans 8:28

God is working on it! . . . and for our good. Don't take it upon yourself to give Him a time schedule or suggest the tools He is to use to get the job done.

"Casting all your care upon him; for he careth for you."

I Peter 5:7

The Lord has the answer to every problem of life, and the thing that really counts is that He cares.

"Get thee hence, and turn thee eastward, and hide thyself by the brook Cherith, that is before Jordan. And it shall be, that thou shalt drink of the brook; and I have commanded the ravens to feed thee there."

I Kings 17:3,4

On the authority of God's Word, needs can be met by means that will stagger the imagination of man. God can do anything, and today, you can believe Him for a miracle in your life.

"But seek ye first the kingdom of God, and his righteousness; and all these things shall be added unto you."

Matthew 6:33

Once we make Jesus the final authority in our lives, everything else becomes automatic. Let's pray, "Today we accept You as Saviour, and make You Lord. Amen."

———————

"The impotent man answered him, Sir, I have no man, when the water is troubled, to put me into the pool: but while I am coming, another steppeth down before me. Jesus saith unto him, Rise, take up thy bed, and walk."

John 5:7,8

This is a story of a man who allowed Jesus to come into his life and exchange his explanation into an experience that put him on his feet. If you are looking for a real happening in your life, He is the one who can do it.

———————

"For with God nothing shall be impossible."

Luke 1:37

This is the way God sees your problem. Turn what faith you have loose in the middle of this great promise and go on to victory. Father, I look to Your Word, and I pray that You will meet the need of this reader, no matter how hopeless it may appear, in the name of Jesus. Amen and thank You.

"That thy trust may be in the Lord, I have made known to thee this day, even to thee. Have not I written to thee excellent things in counsels and knowledge."

Proverbs 22:19,20

Life's answers are lost to us because we keep leaning to our own understanding or taking the advice of those who are as much in the dark as we are. Read the Bible every day and apply it to your everyday need.

"But one thing is needful."

Luke 10:42

There is one thing that is truly necessary in life, and that is to have Christ. There are many things in this life that are out of reach, but here is man's greatest need within the reach of all.

"But my God shall supply all your need according to his riches in glory by Christ Jesus."
Philippians 4:19

The unclaimed fortunes of Heaven are waiting to be delivered on earth to people of big faith and great vision. "With God, all things are possible."

"Casting all your care upon him; for he careth for you."
I Peter 5:7

It was never meant for us to bear the burdens of life, but rather, to share them with Him who knows us so well. We live beneath our privileges and above our heads when we seek to carry on without Him.

"And at midnight Paul and Silas prayed, and sang praises unto God: and the prisoners heard them. And suddenly there was a great earthquake, so that the foundations of the prison were shaken: and immediately all the doors were opened, and every one's bands were loosed."
Acts 16:25,26

In the darkest hour of your life, look for the midnight specialist, the Lord Jesus, to open doors and solve your problems.

"And I say unto you, Ask, and it shall be given you; seek, and ye shall find; knock, and it shall be opened unto you."

Luke 11:9

There are no problems that will not surrender to persistent prayer. "Lord, teach us to pray."

"All that the Father giveth me shall come to me; and him that cometh to me I will in no wise cast out."

John 6:37

Whoever you are, whatever your need, the solution will be found in the Saviour. No habit or hurt is too much for Him to heal. You have tried everything else. Why not try Him? "Whosoever will may come."

"For God hath not given us the spirit of fear; but of power, and of love, and of a sound mind."
II Timothy 1:7

The average person is apt to spend more time with his fears than he does with his faith. Father, banish the tormenting fears that come upon us by the power of the Holy Spirit, in Jesus' name. Amen.

"He sent his word, and healed them, and delivered them from their destructions."
Psalms 107:20

The Word of God is the Great Physician in the person of Jesus on a mission of mercy, healing and ministering to all the needs of all the world. Let Him!

"I cried unto the Lord with my voice; with my voice unto the Lord did I make my supplication. I poured out my complaint before him; I shewed before him my trouble."
Psalms 142:1,2

Forget all the formalities and just tell God how you feel. Nor do you need to keep checking to see whether or not you got through. "My ear is not heavy that it cannot hear.'' Jesus said, "If ye shall ask anything in my name, I will do it.''

"But Jesus beheld them, and said unto them, With men this is impossible; but with God all things are possible.''
Matthew 19:26

If you are facing a situation and there is no way out, look up. Ask Him for proof; seek Him for power; apply this word to your worry. "Ye have not because ye ask not.'' Father, meet our impossible needs with Your Almighty power. In Jesus' name. Amen.

"Behold, I am the Lord, the God of all flesh: is there any thing too hard for me?''
Jeremiah 32:27

Weigh your problem over against His promise . . . and believe for the answer! "All things are possible to him that believeth.'' "All power is given unto me in heaven and in earth.''

"O the depth of the riches both of the wisdom and knowledge of God! how unsearchable are his judgments, and his ways past finding out!"

Romans 11:33

With that kind of resource, isn't it regrettable that we continue to live with our problems. God knows everything and can do anything. Look to Him for the answer.

"And, behold, there was a great earthquake: for the angel of the Lord descended from heaven, and came and rolled back the stone from the door, and sat upon it. His countenance was like lightning, and his raiment white as snow: And for fear of him the keepers did shake, and became as dead men."

Matthew 28:2-4

The God who did all of this to raise Jesus from the dead can today lift you up and let you out of whatever is holding you back from a new and abundant life. Rise up in His name. Amen.

"And thou shalt remember all the way which the Lord thy God led thee . . ."

Deuteronomy 8:2

A clear memory of God's past blessings will keep us from panic at the thought of present day problems. He is still the same and is up to any emergency that may come upon you.

"I called upon the Lord in distress: the Lord answered me, and set me in a large place."
Psalms 118.5

In his most distressing moment, the true believer can expect divine deliverance. "He remaineth faithful."

"God is our refuge and strength, a very present help in trouble."
Psalms 46:1

Life presents no problems that Christ cannot solve.

"But my God shall supply all your need according to his riches in glory by Christ Jesus."
Philippians 4:19

We have yet to see what our God can do, and what we can do with Him in us and with us.

"If then God so clothe the grass, which is to day in the field, and to morrow is cast into the oven; how much more will he clothe you, O ye of little faith?"
Luke 12:28

Victory is ours when we remember how much we mean to God. We are products of the providence of a Heavenly Father, fully capable of meeting our earthly needs.

"But my God shall supply all your need according to his riches in glory by Christ Jesus."
Philippians 4:19

If you belong to God, you are entitled to what He has. He invites you to ask for it. "Ask what ye will."

"For the Lord God is a sun and shield: the Lord will give grace and glory: no good thing will he withhold from them that walk uprightly."

Psalms 84:11

God is for us having the good things. We need to get our priorities in order so that we can have them.

". . . pray one for another, that ye may be healed . . ."

James 5:16

Pray this promise! Just now, think of what you have need of and then pray for others who have the same need. In the mighty name of Jesus, my Father, I pray for others and I believe. Amen.

"The silver is mine, and the gold is mine, saith the Lord of hosts."

Haggai 2:8

"For every beast of the forest is mine, and the cattle upon a thousand hills."

Psalms 50:1

We need to cease acting as though God is poor and that He is unaware of our needs and unable to meet them. "Beloved, I wish above all things that thou mayest prosper and be in health, even as thy soul prospereth."

———————

"But seek ye first the kingdom of God, and his righteousness; and all these things shall be added unto you."

Matthew 6:33

It seems like Jesus is saying that once our priorities are in order, answers to our prayers will be automatic.

———————

"Or what man is there of you, whom if his son ask bread, will he give him a stone? Or if he ask a fish, will he give him a serpent? If ye then, being evil, know how to give good gifts unto your

children, how much more shall your Father which is in heaven give good things to them that ask him?
Matthew 7:9-11

Our God who created us will surely do as much for us as we would for our children. With that in mind, believe Him for your miracle. "For with God, nothing shall be impossible."

———————

"Ask, and it shall be given you; seek, and ye shall find; knock, and it shall be opened unto you."

Matthew 7:7

Believe God for anything while believing Him for the best thing. Our Father, take this prayer, in Jesus' name, to bring about miracles that cannot be denied or ignored. Amen.

———————

"Ascribe ye strength unto God: his excellency is over Israel, and his strength is in the clouds."

Psalms 68:34

Look for His strength in the clouds of your life, for it shall surely be there. "I will never leave thee nor forsake thee." Father, be with those in great distress just now, and may they feel Your presence and know that You care and deliver them, in Jesus' name. Amen.

———————

"When I said, My foot slippeth; thy mercy, O Lord, held me up."

Psalms 94:18

He is that close, and He cares. He does rescue us and His mercy endureth forever.

———————

"And it shall come to pass, that before they call, I will answer; and while they are yet speaking, I will hear."

Isaiah 65:24

The Lord is always out in front of us. "He knows the thought and the intent of the heart." Because He wants the best for us, He proceeds to answer many times in advance of our calling. What a Father! — What a Saviour!

"But my God shall supply all your need according to his riches in glory by Christ Jesus."
Philippians 4:19

He is Savior, supplier and soon coming King. Worship Him now. Father, I pray for every need of every reader. Perform miracles in every area of life that cannot be denied or ignored, in Jesus' name. Amen and thank You.

"Call unto me, and I will answer thee, and show thee great and mighty things, which thou knowest not."
Jeremiah 33:3

God can bring to pass any promise that He has made. In this moment, think of your greatest need and let's believe God for the answer. In Jesus' name, oh God, for Your glory and our good, answer our prayer. Amen. We praise You.

"And it shall come to pass in the day that the Lord shall give thee rest from thy sorrow, and from thy fear, and from the hard bondage wherein thou wast made to serve."

Isaiah 14:3

In a moment of time, He can make up for all the hard times. "Casting all your care upon him, for he careth for you."

―――――――――

"Hide not thy face from me in the day when I am in trouble; incline thine ear unto me: in the day when I call answer me speedily."

Psalms 102:2

Feel free to talk to God like that. He understands the language of desperation and He will deliver. I am praying that your prayer will be answered for His glory and your good. Amen.

―――――――――

"And Jesus came and spake unto them, saying, All power is given unto me in heaven and in earth."

Matthew 28:18

The next time you think about your big problem, take another look at Him who has

all power. Apply that power to the problem.
No problem!

"Who his own self bare our sins in his own
body on the tree, that we, being dead to sins,
should live unto righteousness: by whose stripes
ye were healed."

I Peter 2:24

Move out on faith, accept all He has accomplished, and receive all He has promised.
He said, "I will never leave thee nor forsake
thee." Father, grant great miracles in all our
lives as we apply simple faith against all our
needs, in Jesus' name. Amen. Thank You.

"Behold, I am the Lord, the God of all flesh:
is there any thing too hard for me?"

Jeremiah 32:27

Put your biggest problem up against
this great promise of the Lord and watch it
dissolve. Father, in Jesus' name, please meet
this reader with a miracle right now I pray,
Amen.

"Who his own self bare our sins in his own body on the tree, that we, being dead to sins, should live unto righteousness: by whose stripes ye were healed."

I Peter 2:24

Calvary truly covered it all. Why will we wait when so much is waiting for us? Whatever the problem, He is the answer.

"Be not ye therefore like unto them: for your Father knoweth what things ye have need of, before ye ask him."

Matthew 6:8

Take time to thank Him for the needs met upon request, but also for the many met without request. "But my God shall supply all your need according to his riches in glory by Christ Jesus."

"Behold the fowls of the air: for they sow not, neither do they reap, nor gather into barns; yet your heavenly Father feedeth them. Are ye not much better than they?"

Matthew 6:26

The Lord calls us to bird watching to build up our faith. The lessons we learn will lift us up above our own circumstances and give us a greater appreciation and love for our Creator, who gave us life to enjoy, not endure. Thanks, Jesus for the illustration.

"Teach me thy way, O Lord; I will walk in thy truth: unite my heart to fear thy name."
Psalms 86:11

God is interested in needs. Prayer is the way to get them met. When was the last time that you spent some time in prayer? "If ye shall ask anything in my name, I will do it."

"Come unto me, all ye that labour and are heavy laden, and I will give you rest."
Matthew 11:28

Think of all the peace we forfeit because we will not act on this promise. Father, we come with our burdens and we believe You for miracles, in Jesus' name. Amen, and thank You.

"I am the good shepherd: the good shepherd giveth his life for the sheep."

John 10:11

On the cross, Jesus identified Himself with every sin, struggle and crisis of life. In this moment, receive that as a cure for every problem and go free forever. Father, I ask for salvation for everyone and liberation from every hurt and habit that may be harassing them. In Jesus' name, Amen.

_____

Peace - Happiness - Joy....

Peace - Happiness - Joy

"And the way of peace have they not known."

Romans 3:17

Man is continuously reaching out for peace while leaving God out of his plans. "Peace on earth, good will toward men" is still accompanied only by the presence of Christ.

"Happy is that people, that is in such a case: yea, happy is that people, whose God is the Lord."

Psalms 144:15

Here is where happiness is! Isn't it strange that we have searched for it in so many other things and places? Father, forgive us, in Jesus name. Amen.

"But, the fruit of the Spirit is . . . joy . . ."
Galatians 5:22

It is not where we are, or who we are, but what and whose we are that makes us joyful.

"Restore unto me the joy of thy salvation. . . ."

Psalms 51:12

Do you have the same joy, peace, and compassion for others that once ruled your spirit? If not, then turn to Him who hath begun a good work in you and is able to revive that which you seemed to have lost. Nothing but sin can take away the Christian's joy.

"Therefore being justified by faith, we have peace with God through our Lord Jesus Christ."

Romans 5:1

There is no real peace inside, outside of Christ. He gives the peace that passeth all understanding. Peace that the world cannot give or take away.

"For unto us a child is born, unto us a son is given: and the government shall be upon his shoulder: and his name shall be called Wonderful, Counseller, The mighty God, The everlasting Father, The Prince of Peace."

Isaiah 9:6

In our search for peace, it seems that we have called in everyone but the real peacemaker. "My peace I give unto you. . ." Perhaps we need to make peace with God before we can talk peace with man.

———————

"Blessed are the peacemakers: for they shall be called the children of God."

Matthew 5:9

In our anxiety for peace with man, let us not pass a still greater obligation—that of making peace with Our Maker.

———————

"For I delivered unto you first of all that which I also received, how that Christ died for our sins according to the scriptures."

I Corinthians 15:3

We must acknowledge personally that He died for our sins, if we are to have any personal peace.

———————————

"Then he said unto them, Go your way, eat the fat, and drink the sweet, and send portions unto them for whom nothing is prepared: for this day is holy unto our Lord: neither be ye sorry; for the joy of the Lord is your strength."

Nehemiah 8:10

True happiness comes from knowing the Lord, and true strength comes from the knowledge that He is with you, in you, and for you. "I will never leave thee nor forsake thee."

———————————

"Happy are thy men, happy are these thy servants, which stand continually before thee, and that hear thy wisdom."

I Kings 10:8

Don't condemn the emotional Christians. Perhaps they have found a joy that belongs to us all, but which we have heretofore ignored or overlooked. God's people ought to be the happiest and the busiest people on earth.

———————————

"These things have I spoken unto you, that my joy might remain in you, and that your joy might be full."

John 15:11

The Christianity that Jesus talked about and provided for called for His people to be overjoyed, not overbearing nor overburdened.

———————

"And let the peace of God rule in your hearts, to the which also ye are called in one body; and be ye thankful."

Colossians 3:15

There can be no peace in our hearts until we make up our minds to come to terms with God. "My peace I give unto you."

———————

"And I will give them an heart to know me, that I am the Lord: and they shall be my people, and I will be their God: for they shall return unto me with their whole heart."

Jeremiah 24:7

There is no peace of mind without whole-hearted surrender. "When ye seek for me with your whole heart, ye shall find me."

———————

"Peace I leave with you, my peace I give unto you: not as the world giveth, give I unto you. Let not your heart be troubled, neither let it be afraid."

John 14:27

The peace that counts is found at an altar of prayer, not at a table. Let's get back to the Bible . . . and God.

"But godliness with contentment is great gain."

I Timothy 6:6

Do you ever see people like that? Perhaps they have read this and believed it. Let's join them!

"And, having made peace through the blood of his cross, by him to reconcile all things unto himself; by him, I say, whether they be things in earth, or things in heaven."

Colossians 1:20

Just as the price of peace for every war has been the shedding of blood—so with eternal peace for our salvation. It was paid for by the blood of Jesus Christ, God's only begotten Son.

"Now the Lord of peace himself give you peace always by all means. The Lord be with you all."

II Thessalonians 3:16

He is the Peacemaker and the Peacekeeper. Turn all of the conflicts of your life over to Him. "My peace I give unto you."

"Therefore being justified by faith, we have peace with God through our Lord Jesus Christ."
Romans 5:1

Think of it. Peace with God. Without that, everything else in the world is reduced to nothing. Jesus said, "My peace I give unto you...." By all means, take it.

"Therefore being justified by faith, we have peace with God through our Lord Jesus Christ."
Romans 5:1

Do you have peace with God? In this moment through Jesus, you can. Take it by faith forever. Receive and rejoice!

"Thou lovest righteousness, and hatest wickedness: therefore God, thy God, hath annointed thee with the oil of gladness above thy fellows.''

Psalms 45:7

Make it a point to love the good things of life. The Lord will make it a point to see that you are rewarded. "No good thing will he withhold from them that walk uprightly."

———

"Then the same day at evening, being the first day of the week, when the doors were shut where the disciples were assembled for fear of the Jews, came Jesus and stood in the midst, and saith unto them, Peace be unto you.''

John 20:19

In a world of strife, the Savior is still the Peacemaker. "My peace I give unto you, not as the world giveth give I unto you - let not your heart be troubled and neither let it be afraid." Father, give peace to every troubled heart just now, in Jesus' name, Amen.

———

"My heart is fixed, O God, my heart is fixed: I will sing and give praise."

Psalms 57:7

It's a great day in our lives when our hearts are right with God and our minds are at peace. Out of this experience will come joy unspeakable. It can happen today as we invite the Prince of Peace in. "My peace I give unto you."

"These things I have spoken unto you, that in me ye might have peace. In the world ye shall have tribulation: but be of good cheer; I have overcome the world."

John 16:33

The Lord doesn't want us to be under the circumstances, but an overcomer with Him. "My grace is sufficient for thee." Whatever the problem, He is the answer.

"Peace I leave with you, my peace I give unto you: not as the world giveth, give I unto you. Let not your heart be troubled, neither let it be afraid."

John 14:27

He gives the peace "that passes all understanding that the world cannot give, neither can it take away." Why don't we receive it? Father, in Jesus' great name, we receive the peace that You have promised. We also pray for peace world-wide. Amen. Thank You.

"Yet I will rejoice in the Lord, I will joy in the God of my salvation."

Habakkuk 3:18

There are good times in God's service. He planned it that way. Give Him praise. "Rejoice in the Lord alway: and again I say, Rejoice." Not only prayer but praise is mountain moving.

Praising God....

Praising God

"Praise ye the Lord. Praise God in his sanctuary: praise him in the firmament of his power."

Psalms 150:1

When was the last time you heard praise in the sanctuary - that is to God! Praise ye the Lord. "Let everything that hath breath praise the Lord."

"Praise the Lord, O Jerusalem; praise thy God, O Zion. For he hath strengthened the bars of thy gates; he hath blessed thy children within thee. He maketh peace in thy borders, and filleth thee with the finest of the wheat."

Psalms 147:12-14

There is a time to shorten our petitions and lengthen our praise. We live in such a time. Praise ye the Lord!

"Who led thee through that great and terrible wilderness, wherein were fiery serpents, and scorpions, and drought, where there was no water; who brought thee forth water out of the rock of flint."

Deuteronomy 8:15

If you have been out there in the wilderness, don't forget the guide who led you through it. Praise God from whom all blessings flow. Father, we praise You.

"And were continually in the temple, praising and blessing God."

Luke 24:53

It's still true that more time in the temple and less time for the temporal makes for victorious living. "I was glad when they said unto me, let us go into the house of the Lord."

". . . for he is thy Lord; and worship thou him."

Psalms 45:11

Only One deserves our worship. Only One is worthy of our worship. The praise life will wear out the self life. "When ye seek me with your whole heart, ye shall find me."

"Sing unto the Lord, bless his name; shew forth his salvation from day to day."

Psalms 96:2

Don't let your religion be a weekend matter for a weekend religion is a weak one. But every day, by work and by life, show forth His salvation.

———

". . . rejoice in every good thing which the Lord thy God hath given unto thee."

Deuteronomy 26:11

Have you thought to thank Him recently? Do you feel that the good things which you enjoy are accidental and through some effort of your own? Who gives you the power and wisdom and strength to get gain? Acknowledge the hand of God in your life now that it may be well with you in the future. "Let every thing that hath breath praise the Lord."

———

"In everything give thanks . . ."

I Thessalonians 5:18

Ingratitude is one of the great sins of our day. Follow this prescription and see if

the praise life won't wear down the self life.
"Be ye thankful."

"Blessed be the Lord, who daily loadeth us
with benefits, even the God of our salvation.
Selah."

Psalms 68:19

Have you stopped petitioning God long
enough to praise Him lately? Count your
blessings - if you can!

"I was glad when they said unto me, Let
us go into the house of the Lord."

Psalms 122:1

Do you go to church to get it over with
or to become a part of it? Let the worship service become a personal experience and go
forward in your faith.

"O give thanks unto the Lord, for he is good: for his mercy endureth for ever."

Psalms 107:1

Give Him thanks for what even seems to be reverses today. Tomorrow you may discover that in His wise providence, they were advancements. "All things work together for good to them that love the Lord . . ."

"Speaking to yourselves in psalms and hymns and spiritual songs, singing and making melody in your heart to the Lord."

Ephesians 5:19

There is a lot to be said about talking to yourself and then there is a great deal more to be said about talking to God. Every day will be a better one if we will do both.

"Blessed be the Lord, who daily loadeth us with benefits, even the God of our salvation."

Psalms 68:19

It is not right to give thanks once a year for blessings received every day. "Sing forth the honor of his name! Make his praise glorious."

———————

"Oh give thanks to the Lord of lords: for his mercy endureth for ever."

Psalms 136:3

Prayer unlocks the door. Praise keeps it open. "Praise God from whom all blessings flow."

———————

"Praise the Lord; for the Lord is good: sing praises unto his name; for it is pleasant."

Psalms 135:3

Praise should be a definite part of our life every day. It probably would surprise us if we knew how much answered prayer depends on our attitude of praise to God. "Be thankful unto him, and bless his name."

———————

"Praise ye the Lord. Sing unto the Lord a new song, and his praise in the congregation of saints."

Psalms 149:1

There is not only power in prayer but in praise. Have you ever thanked Him for things that appear to be going against you as well as what seems to be going for you? "In everything give thanks: for this is the will of God in Christ Jesus concerning you."

"Fear not, O land; be glad and rejoice: for the Lord will do great things."

Joel 2:21

So many times the victory is in the rejoicing rather than in the pleading. Thank Him in advance now; and acknowledge that He is able to do above and beyond what you can ask or think.

"And one of them, when he saw that he was healed, turned back, and with a loud voice glorified God, And fell down on his face at his feet, giving him thanks: and he was a Samaritan."

Luke 17:15,16

We all go to Him in prayer, but how many times do we return to Him in thanks? And we hear a lot about prayer lists, but when was the last time you heard of a praise list? It is a good thing to give thanks unto the Lord.

———————

"Who redeemeth thy life from destruction; who crowneth thee with lovingkindness and tender mercies."

Psalms 103:4

How about giving God a word of thanks for what He did that you didn't see. Thank You Lord!

———————

"It is a good thing to give thanks unto the Lord, and to sing praises unto thy name, O most High."

Psalms 92:1

Not only in times of abundance but in times of trials and adversity, it is good to give thanks. "In everything give thanks: for this is the will of God in Christ Jesus concerning you."

———————

"Let all those that seek thee rejoice and be glad in thee: let such as love thy salvation say continually, The Lord be magnified.''

Psalms 40:16

Let's get our priorities straight. Make big of God! Man was never meant to be exalted and God ignored. God will not share His glory with another.

––––––––

''Praise ye the Lord. Praise God in his sanctuary: praise him in the firmament of his power. Praise him for his mighty acts: praise him according to his excellent greatness . . . Let every thing that hath breath praise the Lord. Praise ye the Lord.''

Psalms 150:1,2,6

For a well rounded devotional life to God, it is obvious from His Word that the life of praise to Him should have equal time with our prayer life.

––––––––

''Blessed be the Lord, who daily loadeth us with benefits, even the God of our salvation. Selah.''

Psalms 68:19

We are defeated the moment we allow ourselves to start listing our burdens instead of counting our blessings. Note too, this is a "daily" matter with God to bestow His benefits . . . it should also be a daily matter with us to praise Him. "Lord, we do praise thee". "Bless the Lord, O my soul, and forget not all his benefits."

"That they all may be one; as thou, Father, art in me, and I in thee, that they also may be one in us: that the world may believe that thou hast sent me."

John 17:21

Why don't we quit waving church labels and just worship the Lord? This is what Jesus prayed for long ago. He is the way, the truth and life - the answer, the difference, everything. Let's follow Him together.

"Let my mouth be filled with thy praise and with thy honour all the day."

Psalms 71:8

If you have faced something that has not surrendered to prayer, try praising God for it. "I will hope continually, and will yet praise thee more and more."

"Blessed be the Lord God of Israel for ever and ever. And all the people said, Amen, and praised the Lord."

I Chronicles 16:36

It should be the normal thing, not unusual, for all of us to so respond when we think of His goodness. Praise ye the Lord!

"This is the day which the Lord hath made; we will rejoice and be glad in it."

Psalms 118:24

He has made the day. Praising Him for it makes it better! From the rising of the sun to the going down thereof, His praise shall continually be in my mouth.

"Great is the Lord, and greatly to be praised; and his greatness is unsearchable."

Psalms 145:3

Once we start praising Him, we can
never really stop because there is no end to
His greatness and our reason to be grateful.

"Sing unto the Lord with thanksgiving; sing
praise upon the harp unto our God: Who covereth
the heaven with clouds, who prepareth rain for
the earth, who maketh grass to grow upon the
mountains. He giveth to the beast his food, and
to the young ravens which cry."

Psalms 147:7-9

A lot of confusion as to what happened to our prayers would clear up if we could
only give a little more time in praising God.
"Praise ye the Lord." Father, I praise Thee
for health and happiness, for family and
friends, the joy of Your service, Your Word,
Church and most of all, for salvation and the
baptism of Your Spirit.

"We took sweet counsel together, and walked unto the house of God in company."
Psalms 55:14

More time in God's house will bring about better times in our house.

"In everything give thanks: for this is the will of God in Christ Jesus concerning you."
I Thessalonians 5:18

No matter how you feel or how things look, go ahead and give Him thanks and expect a change. "It is a good thing to give thanks unto the Lord."

"When thou hast eaten and art full, then thou shalt bless the Lord thy God for the good land which he hath given thee."
Deuteronomy 8:10

Praise is the pause that refreshes. Take time to thank God for the food . . . millions would like to do it for you.

"Let all those that seek thee rejoice and be glad in thee: and let such as love thy salvation say continually, Let God be magnified."

Psalms 70:4

We must be careful to hate nothing but sin, and exalt none but God. Oh Lord, we praise Thee!

"I have blotted out, as a thick cloud, thy transgressions, and, as a cloud, thy sins: return unto me; for I have redeemed thee."

Isaiah 44:22

Praise the Lord! A God who will do all of that is worthy of our attention and allegiance forever. Whatever the problem, He is the answer.

"And of Joseph he said, Blessed of the Lord be his land, for the precious things of heaven, for the dew, and for the deep that coucheth beneath, And for the precious fruits brought forth by the sun, and for the precious things put forth by the moon."

Deuteronomy 33:13,14

How often do we praise Him for life personally, and for the production of the land at our disposal. All the glory is due to Thy name, Our Father, and we praise You in Jesus' name. Amen.

"And thou shalt rejoice in every good thing which the Lord thy God hath given unto thee, and unto thine house, thou, and the Levite, and the stranger that is among you."

Deuteronomy 26:11

Have you set aside your want list long enough to run a praise inventory to detail the blessing of God on you and your household? God said this is a good thing to do.

"It is a good thing to give thanks unto the Lord, and to sing praises unto thy name, O most High."

Psalms 92:1

Be as anxious to praise Him as you are to petition Him. The Bible says it's a good thing. It is also the right thing. "Let everything that hath breath praise the Lord."

"And in that day shall ye say, Praise the Lord, call upon his name, declare his doings among the people, make mention that his name is exhalted."

Isaiah 12:4

Praise Him for what He has done, and in advance for what you expect Him to do. What a volume of praise would rise today if for one moment we would thank Him for past blessings. I praise Thee, oh God. Praise Father, Son, and Holy Ghost. Amen.

Prayer....

Prayer

"Call unto me, and I will answer thee, and shew thee great and mighty things, which thou knowest not."

Jeremiah 33:3

The world has yet to see in full what God is willing to do in response to prevailing prayer. "With God, all things are possible."

"Thou calledst in trouble, and I delivered thee; I answered thee in the secret place of thunder: I proved thee at the waters of Meribah. Selah."

Psalms 81:7

Hold up that petition for a moment. Remember, and be thankful for the prayers that He has answered in the past. May all our prayers be preceded by praise.

"In my distress I called upon the Lord, and cried to my God: and he did hear my voice out of his temple, and my cry did enter into his ears."

II Samuel 22:7

Much of life is taken with trying to be heard of man, while God in Heaven waits to give us a ready audience any time we lift our voice. "I sought the Lord and he heard me and delivered me . . ."

"And his name through faith in his name hath made this man strong, whom ye see and know: yea, the faith which is by him hath given him this perfect soundness in the presence of you all."

Acts 3:16

We must remember that it's in the authority of Jesus' name that we can expect answers to our prayers. "If ye shall ask anything in my name, I will do it."

"If ye then, being evil, know how to give good gifts unto your children, how much more shall your Father which is in heaven give good things to them that ask him?"

Matthew 7:11

We should not only be courageous in our asking, but confident of His answer.

"Lord, in trouble have they visited thee, they poured out a prayer when thy chastening was upon them."

Isaiah 26:16

Very often, it is true, that the only time we look to Christ is when we get in a corner. A few moments with the Lord will keep us from the anxious hours ahead.

"For this cause I bow my knees unto the Father of our Lord Jesus Christ."

Ephesians 3:14

More bowing of the knees means less bowing to the world. You can go all the way to the top on your knees. Prayer is priceless. "Pray without ceasing."

"And he prayed again, and the heaven gave rain, and the earth brought forth her fruit."

James 5:18

The Lord hears us when we pray, but sometimes tests our sincerity by how often we pray. Don't give up, and God will never let you down.

". . . God, who answered me in the day of my distress . . ."

Genesis 35:3

He is still in the prayer-answering business. Whatever your grounds for asking, remember you must be on praying ground. Pray hardest when it's hardest to pray.

————————

"Again I say unto you, That if two of you shall agree on earth as touching any thing that they shall ask, it shall be done for them of my Father which is in heaven."

Matthew 18:19

All you need to have a successful prayer meeting is for two people to agree that God is able.

————————

"Now I beseech you, brethren, for the Lord Jesus Christ's sake, and for the love of the Spirit, that ye strive together with me in your prayers to God for me."

Romans 15:30

Prayer is the greatest contribution that we can make to the life of another. "Brethren, pray for us."

————————

"For every one that asketh receiveth; and he that seeketh findeth; and to him that knocketh it shall be opened."

Matthew 7:8

Here is a three-fold formula for a successful prayer life. The turning point of our lives is when we truly turn everything over to Him in prayer. Pray on! He will not fail thee.

———————

"Come now, and let us reason together, saith the Lord: though your sins be as scarlet, they shall be as white as snow; though they be red like crimson, they shall be as wool."

Isaiah 1:18

More time should be spent in taking our sins to God instead of brooding over them. "If we confess our sins, he is faithful and just to forgive us."

———————

"When my soul fainted within me I remembered the Lord: and my prayer came in unto thee, into thine holy temple."

Jonah 2:7

Why is it that we so often wait until we get down and out before we look up? "Him that cometh to me I will in no wise cast out."

"And Samuel said, Gather all Israel to Mizpeh, and I will pray for you unto the Lord."
I Samuel 7:5

In our busy petitions for ourselves, we should stop long enough to exercise the glorious privilege of praying for each other. "Pray one for another."

"Confess your faults one to another, and pray one for another, that ye may be healed. The effectual fervent prayer of a righteous man availeth much."
James 5:16

It is good to be pulling for someone, but much better to be praying for them. Right now, take a moment to lift a prayer for someone. It could mean the difference in their life here and their future in the hereafter.

"If ye shall ask anything in my name, I will do it "

John 14:14

It's all in the authority of His name and in the power of His might. If Jesus is your Saviour, you are a member of God's family and have a right to His fortune which is limitless. Ask big and believe!

"And all things, whatsoever ye shall ask in prayer, believing, ye shall receive."

Matthew 21:22

Go up against your greatest problem with this simple prayer pattern and look for answers, for they are sure to come. Jesus said, ". . . I will do it."

"And at midnight Paul and Silas prayed, and sang praises unto God: and the prisoners heard them. And suddenly there was a great earthquake, so that the foundations of the prison were shaken: and immediately all the doors were opened, and every one's bands were loosed."

Acts 16:25,26

He is still opening doors in response to simple faith and prevailing prayer. Let us remember prisoners in every part of the world and every walk of life.

———————

"And whatsoever ye shall ask in my name, that will I do, that the Father may be glorified in the Son."

John 14:13

Here is a promise for the man who will be daring enough to believe that the Lord is able to do what He said. Turn your world around. Start now to take Him at His Word.

———————

"For I said in my haste, I am cut off from before thine eyes: nevertheless thou heardest the voice of my supplications when I cried unto thee."

Psalms 31:22

Many times in our impatience, we all have felt that we were cut off from Heaven, only to discover that there was a time span we were unaware of . . . and the Lord was on the line all along doing it His way. Keep talking to God. Don't let anything break down the line of communication. You're getting through, and God is coming through!

———————

"When thou saidst, Seek ye my face; my heart said unto thee, Thy face, Lord, will I seek."
Psalms 27:8

A prayer life that will reach God and touch humanity calls for something a great deal more than a casual approach. "Wait on the Lord."

_____

"Continue in prayer, and watch in the same with thanksgiving."
Colossians 4:2

Our prayers should always be followed by anticipation and gratitude. "When ye pray . . . believe and ye shall receive."

_____

"Watch ye and pray, lest ye enter into temptation. The spirit truly is ready, but the flesh is weak."
Mark 14:38

Lack of prayer leaves a person open to many suggestions and little spirit to face them. A man out of touch with God will find evil pretty close at hand.

_____

". . . one of his disciples said unto him, Lord, teach us to pray . . ."

Luke 11:1

It would seem that the closer a man is to the Lord, the more he sees his need of prayer. Prayer is a personal inventory of our spiritual needs and a private audience with Him "who sticketh closer than a brother."

———————

". . . Come up hither, and I will shew thee things which must be hereafter."

Revelation 4:1

You can't live in the valley and see very far. Mountain-top experiences are for knee-bending Christians.

———————

"Then came she and worshipped him, saying, Lord, help me."

Matthew 15:25

Keep looking up, and the Lord will never let you down. Prayer changes things.

———————

"And Jacob was left alone; and there wrestled a man with him until the breaking of the day . . and Jacob called the name of the place Peniel: for I have seen God face to face, and my life is preserved."

Genesis 32:24,30

No man spends a night before God without victory in the morning. Prayer changes things.

———————

"Giving thanks always for all things unto God and the Father in the name of our Lord Jesus Christ."

Ephesians 5:20

We are not only to pray in His name, but to give thanks in His name.

———————

"But thou, when thou prayest, enter into thy closet, and when thou hast shut thy door, pray to thy Father which is in secret; and thy Father which seeth in secret shall reward thee openly."

Matthew 6:6

Every word that we speak is recorded. Every prayer that we pray is rewarded. God said, "My ear is not heavy that it cannot hear."

———————

"Ask, and it shall be given you; seek, and ye shall find; knock, and it shall be opened unto you."

Matthew 7:7

Don't give up! Keep your petition with praise before God. I join with them, my Father, in Jesus name, that their prayer will be answered in Your will and time and for their good and Your glory. Amen.

_____

"After this manner therefore pray ye: Our Father which art in heaven, Hallowed be thy name. Thy kingdom come. Thy will be done in earth, as it is in heaven. Give us this day our daily bread. And forgive us our debts, as we forgive our debtors. And lead us not into temptation, but deliver us from evil: For thine is the kingdom, and the power, and the glory, for ever. Amen."

Matthew 6:9-13

Don't try to analyze or sermonize on this prayer. Just gather up all your problems and simply, slowly, and reverently repeat it. Let it be a daily part of you. In it, you are going to God in the words and in the name of His Son. You are bound to get results.

_____

"And the publican, standing afar off, would not lift up so much as his eyes unto heaven, but smote upon his breast, saying, God be merciful to me a sinner."

Luke 18:13

Here is the prayer that brings the peace. Pray it now! When we acknowledge to God what we are, He immediately shows us what He will do. Jesus said, "Him that cometh to me I will in no wise cast out."

"For if ye forgive men their trespasses, your heavenly Father will also forgive you: But if ye forgive not men their trespasses, neither will your Father forgive your trespasses."

Matthew 6:14,15

Could this be what has happened to some of our prayers?...lost between these two verses!

"Thou shalt make thy prayer unto him, and he shall hear thee, and thou shalt pay thy vows."

Job 22:27

What a privilege it is to be heard by the One who has the whole world in His hands. His ear is not heavy that it cannot hear. His hand is not shortened that it cannot save. Pray on. Believe only!

"And it shall come to pass, that before they call, I will answer; and while they are yet speaking, I will hear."

Isaiah 65:24

A prayer thought seems to be as good as a prayer said. God is always out in front of us. Pray boldly, believe big. He is able. Take your family to church. Pray for God's servant. God will bless you.

"I love them that love me; and those that seek me early shall find me."

Proverbs 8:17

What kind of priority does prayer have? "Seek ye first the kingdom of God, and his righteousness; and all these things shall be added unto you."

"Then shalt thou call, and the Lord shall answer; thou shalt cry, and he shall say, Here I am. If thou take away from the midst of thee the yoke, the putting forth of the finger, and speaking vanity."

Isaiah 58:9

Look at this tremendous and tender communication that we can have with the Father through Jesus Christ, His Son. Why don't we pray more?

"And when he had considered the thing, he came to the house of Mary the mother of John, whose surname was Mark; where many were gathered together praying."

Acts 12:12

There is no meeting like a real prayer meeting. What a privilege to pray for one another. I want to pray for whatever is holding you back or getting you down. Oh my Father, if it is a habit or a hurt, a disease or a devil, or whatever is oppressing this reader today, I ask You to deliver them in complete victory, in Jesus' name. Amen.

"And God said to Solomon, Because this was in thine heart, and thou hast not asked riches, wealth, or honour, nor the life of thine enemies, neither yet hast asked long life; but hast asked wisdom and knowledge for thyself, that thou mayest judge my people, over whom I have made thee king: Wisdom and knowledge is granted unto thee; and I will give thee riches, and wealth, and honour, such as none of the kings have had that have been before thee, neither shall there any after thee have the like.''

II Chronicles 1:11,12

All of this followed when Solomon simply asked of the Lord, ''Give thy servant an understanding heart . . .'' Perhaps our prayers should be as unselfish. Why don't we pray the same prayer?

''If I regard iniquity in my heart, the Lord will not hear me.''

Psalms 66:18

Could this be where all of our unanswered prayers are bogged down? We alone can clear the line. Until then, it may be that God has us on hold.

Rebuking Satan....

Rebuking Satan

"Submit yourselves therefore to God. Resist the devil, and he will flee from you."

James 4:7

Speak up to the devil in the name of Jesus. "Greater is he that is in you, than he that is in the world." Jesus said, "I am with you alway."

"Fear not: for I am with thee: I will bring thy seed from the east, and gather thee from the west."

Isaiah 43:5

To know that He is with us! Isn't that great? The further word is, "If God be for us, who can be against us." Praise God! We win!

"And Jesus returned in the power of the Spirit into Galilee: and there went out a fame of him through all the region round about. And he taught in their synagogues, being glorified of all."

Luke 4:14,15

As with Jesus, so it is with us. After the struggle with the enemy, there is strength. "Greater is he that is in you, than he that is in the world."

"Jesus answered them, Verily, verily, I say unto you, Whosoever committeth sin is the servant of sin."

John 8:34

Sin is a hard boss to work for. Long hours, broken hearts, worried minds, and a multitude of bitter memories are the products of the devil. "The wages of sin is death." Be no longer the servant of sin when there is complete release in Christ.

"Be not overcome of evil, but overcome evil with good."

Romans 12:21

Evil has never been a match for goodness. To be an overcomer, you have to overcome a few things. Let the good in your life be so pronounced that if people speak ill of you, no one will believe them.

". . . Why sleep ye? rise and pray, lest ye enter into temptation."

Luke 22:46

People need to be wide-awake and Spirit-filled, and then use common sense to avoid the snares of the devil.

"And they put away the strange gods from among them, and served the Lord . . ."

Judges 10:16

There are a lot of old and strange gods waiting in the shadows of our lives in search of new subjects. They leave only when the true and living God is given the place of prominence in our hearts.

"For the wages of sin is death; but the gift of God is eternal life through Jesus Christ our Lord."

Romans 6:23

Sin pays off . . . in bitter memories, heartache, shame, lost lives and souls. Christ is the way back and up. Jesus said, "I am the way, the truth, and the life: no man cometh to the Father, but by me."

"Ye are of God, little children, and have overcome them: because greater is he that is in you, than he that is in the world."

I John 4:4

We come to master the problems from without when we learn to appropriate power from within. "Nothing shall be impossible unto you."

———————

"For whatsoever is born of God overcometh the world: and this is the victory that overcometh the world, even our faith."

I John 5:4

The need of the hour is for more overcoming Christians with a song and fewer overbearing ones with a sigh.

———————

"My son, if sinners entice thee, consent thou not."

Proverbs 1:10

Say "no" to sin, and the Lord will give you the strength to stand by your decision. "Greater is he that is in you, than he that is in the world."

———————

"Then saith Jesus unto him, Get thee hence, Satan: for it is written, Thou shalt worship the Lord thy God, and him only shalt thou serve. Then the devil leaveth him, and, behold, angels came and ministered unto him."

Matthew 4:10,11

There is a liberation of our spirit that comes only from looking up to the Lord and speaking up to the devil. "Resist the devil and he will flee from you." We overcome by the "word of our testimony and the blood of the Lamb." Thank you, Lord, for the power of Your blood and the might of Your Word! Amen.

———————

"Be not overcome of evil, but overcome evil with good."

Romans 12:21

Keep firing away with good. Someday evil will surrender. "A soft answer turneth away wrath."

———————

"Put on the whole armour of God, that ye may be able to stand against the wiles of the devil."

Ephesians 6:11

A Christian must fortify himself with the Word of God, exercise his faith, and walk in the Spirit. All of this is made easy with the one simple act of allowing Jesus His rightful place in our lives. "Greater is he that is in you, than he that is in the world."

"Be sober, be vigilant; because your adversary the devil, as a roaring lion, walketh about, seeking whom he may devour."

I Peter 5:8

He is out there to devour your time, talents, your home, heart and eternal soul. The only language he understands is our true commitment to Jesus Christ. Today, make that commitment and walk on in confidence. "Lo, I am with you alway."

"And the God of peace shall bruise Satan under your feet shortly. The grace of our Lord Jesus Christ be with you. Amen."

Romans 16:20

Take this as your own promise of the power of God soon to be demonstrated in your life. "Greater is he that is in you, than he that is in the world."

"Submit yourselves therefore to God. Resist the devil, and he will flee from you."

James 4:7

With the resistance will come the release. The power of Jesus breaks the bondage of sin. "The Lord knoweth how to deliver the godly out of temptation."

Salvation....

Salvation

"Jesus saith unto him, I am the way, the truth, and the life: no man cometh unto the Father, but by me."

John 14:6

Here is the way to God! Why go on without Him? The plan of salvation is simple, but must be taken seriously now.

"Neither is there salvation in any other: for there is none other name under heaven given among men, whereby we must be saved."

Acts 4:12

Contrary to what so many seem to believe, salvation is in neither the church nor a cause, but through Christ alone. Jesus said, "I am the way."

". . . Verily I say unto you, Except ye be converted, and become as little children, ye shall not enter into the kingdom of heaven."

Matthew 18:3

Conversion is something more than surrounding your life with good works, religious thought and practice, or even the vain attempt to keep the law. It is a surrender of your will and way and a submission to the complete takeover by Christ.

"Behold, I stand at the door, and knock: if any man hear my voice, and open the door, I will come in to him, and will sup with him, and he with me."

Revelation 3:20

What if suddenly you felt the silence of the departure of His presence, never to return again? "My spirit will not always strive with man." Answer the door now, and invite Him into the living room, the place where you live, and let Him take over for life.

"Neither is there salvation in any other: for there is none other name under heaven given among men, whereby we must be saved."

Acts 4:12

Christ is the only door to eternal life and only unbelief can close it. "Believe on the Lord Jesus Christ and thou shalt be saved."

"But if we walk in the light, as he is in the light, we have fellowship one with another, and the blood of Jesus Christ his Son cleanseth us from all sin."

I John 1:7

There is no blot on your life that can't be cleansed by the blood of Jesus Christ. Believe it and go free. "Though your sins be as scarlet, they shall be as white as snow."

"If we confess our sins, he is faithful and just to forgive us our sins, and to cleanse us from all unrighteousness."

I John 1:9

The man who fails to admit that he is a sinner is certain never to be saved. "All have sinned, and come short of the glory of God."

"I am the door: by me if any man enter in, he shall be saved, and shall go in and out, and find pasture."

John 10:9

Pity the man who finally closes the door in his own face by his failure to take God at

His Word. When He closes the door, no man can open it. When He opens it, no man can close it.

"And it shall come to pass, that whosoever shall call on the name of the Lord shall be saved."
Acts 2:21

God has no favorites. "He is no respector of persons." No sin is too great, no sinner so vile but what He will forgive.

"But God forbid that I should glory, save in the cross of our Lord Jesus Christ . . ."
Galatians 6:14

The cross is a constant reminder that we are helpless in the saving of our own soul. It was Christ who died and rose again to put eternal hope within reach of all.

"For all have sinned, and come short of the glory of God."

Romans 3:23

No sinner is so bad but what he can find refuge in the goodness of God through Christ the Saviour. "Jesus saves."

"Repent ye therefore, and be converted, that your sins may be blotted out, when the times of refreshing shall come from the presence of the Lord."

Acts 3:19

It takes more than a good thought or a kind act to assure a man of eternal life. Our salvation cost Jesus Christ His life, and it will cost us at least our pride in acknowledging that He did it for us.

"I have blotted out, as a thick cloud, thy transgressions, and, as a cloud, thy sins: return unto me; for I have redeemed thee."

Isaiah 44:22

Many times the Lord is far more willing to forgive our sins than we are to forget them. "Whom the Son sets free is free indeed"

"For he saith, I have heard thee in a time accepted, and in the day of salvation have I succoured thee: behold, now is the accepted time; behold, now is the day of salvation."

II Corinthians 6:2

Your eternal salvation is too important to put off until a day that you may never see. "Choose you this day whom ye will serve."

"For that ye ought to say, If the Lord will, we shall live, and do this, or that."

James 4:15

Perhaps it's alright to plan for tomorrow so long as you keep in mind who provides for it. Too many of man's plans have been left on the drawing board because God was left out. "Today is the day of salvation." Make everything else secondary to this.

"For by grace are ye saved through faith; and that not of yourselves: it is the gift of God: Not of works, lest any man should boast."
Ephesians 2:8,9

There is absolutely nothing that you can do to bring about your salvation apart from freely accepting what Jesus has already done. Make no mistake about it, however, there is work to be done after salvation. Work while it is day. The night cometh when no man can work.

———————

"I tell you, Nay: but, except ye repent, ye shall all likewise perish."
Luke 13:3

Jesus was talking to well-disciplined, well-churched, well-read, but all was not well inside because they had not turned from their sins. Repentance is turning around, not slowing down, or standing still. The man who would be saved must do something with Jesus Christ, and then he must do something for Him.

———————

"I have blotted out, as a thick cloud, thy transgressions, and, as a cloud, thy sins: return unto me; for I have redeemed thee."

Isaiah 44:22

In the process of His cleansing, the Saviour never leaves a stain.

"Thanks be unto God for his unspeakable gift."

II Corinthians 9:15

So many have failed to acknowledge the gift, much less thank Him for it. "The gift of God is eternal life through Jesus Christ our Lord."

"For by grace are ye saved through faith; and that not of yourselves: it is the gift of God: Not of works, lest any man should boast."

Ephesians 2:8,9

No man is good enough to save himself, and no man is so bad that God will not do it for him. "Christ died for our sins." "Though your sins be as scarlet, they shall be as white as snow."

"If we confess our sins, he is faithful and just to forgive us our sins, and to cleanse us from all unrighteousness."

I John 1:9

It is as we unburden ourselves to the Lord that He unveils His forgiveness to us. He said, "I will remember their iniquities no more." Believe it now, be happy forever.

"For all have sinned, and come short of the glory of God."

Romans 3:23

The whole world is guilty before God and is up for penalty or pardon, and every man must decide for himself which it will be. The Lord is waiting for your decision now. "Jesus saves."

"So then every one of us shall give account of himself to God."

Romans 14:12

Every man's record is waiting for him at the end of life's day. Old accounts are settled on earth or faced in eternity. Your Heavenly Father will forgive you in Jesus' name.

"For the preaching of the cross is to them that perish foolishness; but unto us which are saved it is the power of God."

I Corinthians 1:18

Take the cross out of the Christian message and we have nothing to say to the world or any solution for our sins. "Christ died for our sins."

"If we say that we have not sinned, we make him a liar, and his word is not in us."

I John 1:10

If we refuse to see ourselves as sinners, we place ourselves outside the reach of the Saviour. He came not to call the righteous but sinners to repentance.

"And they went out, and preached that men should repent."

Mark 6:12

This may not be the most popular message, but no one can deny that it is the most needed. Repentance is turning our backs on the old life and our hearts over to a New Leader.

———————

"For by grace are ye saved through faith; and that not of yourselves: it is the gift of God."

Ephesians 2:8

No amount of work can save you, but just a little faith will write your name in the Book of Life. Scrap your plans and accept His plan of salvation.

———————

"And I saw the dead, small and great, stand before God; and the books were opened: and another book was opened, which is the book of life: and the dead were judged out of those things which were written in the books, according to their works."

Revelation 20:12

Only on this side of the grave can you settle the old account. Don't leave it hanging.

It will follow you into judgment. You can know now about the future. "He that believeth on the Son hath everlasting life. . ."

"Verily, verily, I say unto you, He that heareth my word, and believeth on him that sent me, hath everlasting life, and shall not come into condemnation; but is passed from death unto life."
John 5:24

In an hour when the magic word is transplant, don't lose sight of the Great Physician's ability to transform. One stretches out the old life on earth. The other assures eternal life in Heaven. "If any man be in Christ, he is a new creature."

"That if thou shalt confess with thy mouth the Lord Jesus, and shalt believe in thine heart that God hath raised him from the dead, thou shalt be saved. For with the heart man believeth unto righteousness; and with the mouth confession is made unto salvation."

Romans 10:9,10

The person who really believes in his heart ought to have a bold testimony to go with it. "Let the redeemed of the Lord say so . . ."

"For whatsoever is born of God overcometh the world: and this is the victory that overcometh the world, even our faith."

I John 5:4

Most of us surrender in one way or the other to the call of the world, when all the while, as Christians, we are called to be overcomers. "They overcame by the blood of the Lamb, and the word of their testimony."

"But if we walk in the light, as he is in the light, we have fellowship one with another, and the blood of Jesus Christ his Son cleanseth us from all sin."

I John 1:7

No sin is beyond the cleansing blood of Jesus when we simply come to Him in simple faith, believing. "Christ died for our sins."

"But we are all as an unclean thing, and all our righteousnesses are as filthy rags; and we all do fade as a leaf; and our iniquities, like the wind, have taken us away."

Isaiah 64:6

Don't rely on your righteousness to save you. Outside of Christ, there is no chance. Jesus said . . . "I am the way, the truth, and the life: no man cometh unto the Father, but by Me."

"I said, Lord, be merciful unto me: heal my soul; for I have sinned against thee."

Psalms 41:4

Every man's soul very often stands in need of spiritual repair. The Great Physician, Christ Jesus, stands ready to do the job. He has never lost a patient.

"For Christ also hath once suffered for sins, the just for the unjust, that he might bring us to God, being put to death in the flesh, but quickened by the Spirit."

I Peter 3:18

Why continue to live with sin that Jesus has already died for? Whether you understand it or not, believe it and go free. It is our responsibility to acknowledge our need and His to meet it. This He has already done. Count it as so. Father, we admit that we are sinners and that we cannot save ourselves. However, we acknowledge that Jesus is the Saviour, and we accept Him now in His name. Amen.

". . . be sure your sin will find you out."
Numbers 32:23

Sin, unforgiven by the Lord, is a dangerous thing to have on the loose. Under the blood of Christ, however, sin has lost its dread and power. He will forgive.

". . . Woman, where are those thine accusers? hath no man condemned thee? She said,

No man, Lord. And Jesus said unto her, Neither
do I condemn thee: go, and sin no more.''
John 8:10,11

People who dangle a past before a person ought to be conscious of the Lord's
presence. "If ye forgive not men their
trespasses, neither will your Father forgive
your trespasses."

". . . whosoever believeth on him should
not perish, but have eternal life.''
John 3:15

Our future in the hereafter is decided
in the here and now. "Now is the day of salvation."

". . . now is our salvation nearer than when
we believed. The night is far spent, the day is at
hand . . .''
Romans 13:11,12

Every day brings us closer to the even-
tual meeting with God. Will it be reward or
wrath? Only you can decide that.

"For all have sinned, and come short of the glory of God."

Romans 3:23

Sin is so common, but, thank God, forgiveness is so close. Jesus said, "Him that cometh to me I will in no wise cast out."

————————

"But if we walk in the light, as he is in the light, we have fellowship one with another, and the blood of Jesus Christ his Son cleanseth us from all sin."

I John 1:7

Take a good look at the word "all". There will be times when you will need to remember how deep the cleansing and how much he cares. "He careth for you."

————————

"That if thou shalt confess with thy mouth the Lord Jesus, and shalt believe in thine heart that God hath raised him from the dead, thou shalt be saved. For with the heart man believeth unto righteousness; and with the mouth confession is made unto salvation."

Romans 10:9-10

Salvation is a matter of repentance, believing, and receiving. It should be followed by a lot of sharing.

"For Christ also hath once suffered for sins, the just for the unjust, that he might bring us to God, being put to death in the flesh, but quickened by the Spirit."

I Peter 3:18

Calvary was a one-time sacrifice for our all-time deliverance.

"And their sins and iniquities will I remember no more."

Hebrews 10:17

Talk to the Lord about your sin problem; ask Him for Jesus' sake to forgive you; and then forget it as He does. How can you remember something that no longer exists? Jesus said, "Go in peace, and be whole of thy plague."

"Neither is there salvation in any other: for there is none other name under heaven given among men, whereby we must be saved."

Acts 4:12

It's all in the name of Jesus! To introduce anyone or anything as a substitute or as a means for our salvation is to say that God made a mistake and the death of Jesus was without purpose. "In Him is life."

"That if thou shalt confess with thy mouth the Lord Jesus, and shalt believe in thine heart that God hath raised him from the dead, thou shalt be saved. For with the heart man believeth unto righteousness; and with the mouth confession is made unto salvation."

Romans 10:9,10

Obey the scripture; read it slowly; and be saved forever. The Christian life consists of believing, receiving and sharing. For a truly happy and productive life, take Him into your heart at once and tell it as often as you can! "Ye are my witnesses."

"As far as the east is from the west, so far hath he removed our transgressions from us."

Psalms 103:12

Don't be looking for your past sins; in Christ they are far removed. Just be glad that they are. Father, thank You so much for forgiveness of the past, the privilege of the present and the promise of Your guidance and presence for the future. In Jesus' name, Amen.

———————

"All that the Father giveth me shall come to me; and him that cometh to me I will in no wise cast out."

John 6:37

Cheer up! There is no small print in His great promise. If you have ever had any doubt that He would receive you, read this again and go to Him at once. He loves you. Attend the services in your church . . . feel better all week.

———————

"And they said, Believe on the Lord Jesus Christ, and thou shalt be saved, and thy house."
Acts 16:31

Take this simple message of release and reality, without alteration or addition, to as many people as you can find, and let the Holy Spirit do the rest. "Come . . . and I will give you rest."

"And when he came to himself, he said, How many hired servants of my father's have bread enough and to spare, and I perish with hunger! I will arise and go to my father, and will say unto him, Father, I have sinned against heaven, and before thee."
Luke 15:17,18

It's a great day in a man's life when he finally wakes up to where he is and what he is missing at the Father's house. Your Heavenly Father will forgive you. In Jesus' name, He will!

"He that believeth on him is not condemned: but he that believeth not is condemned already, because he hath not believed in the name of the only begotten Son of God."
John 3:18

Salvation is not a wait-and-see; it is already settled for the believer . . . and the unbeliever. The only way to lift the condemnation is to accept Christ.

———————

"If we confess our sins, he is faithful and just to forgive us our sins, and to cleanse us from all unrighteousness."

I John 1:9

We have too many "nicknames" for sins. We need to call them as God sees them, acknowledge them before Him, and ask Jesus to cover them with His blood. The blood of Jesus Christ, God's Son, cleanseth us from all sin.

———————

"Then delivered he him therefore unto them to be crucified. And they took Jesus, and led him away. And he bearing his cross went forth into a place called the place of a skull, which is called in the Hebrew Golgotha: Where they crucified him, and two other with him, on either side one, and Jesus in the midst."

John 19:16-18

Here is where the price was paid for our pardon, but everyone of us individually must acknowledge it was our sin that caused it before the pardon is valid. "Christ died for our sins."

———————

"And he said unto Jesus, Lord, remember me when thou comest into thy kingdom."

Luke 23:42

The man who makes reservations in this life will have no regrets in the life to come.

———————

"Thou hast set our iniquities before thee, our secret sins in the light of thy countenance."

Psalms 90:8

The beauty of it all is that the One who sees us as we are is willing to make us what we ought to be. In Jesus' name He will. "Him that cometh to me I will in no wise cast out."

". . . Repent ye: for the kingdom of heaven is at hand."

Matthew 3:2

Repentance is turning around and "coming to." "Come unto me, all ye that labor and are heavy laden, and I will give you rest."

"For by grace are ye saved through faith; and that not of yourselves: it is the gift of God: Not of works, lest any man should boast."

Ephesians 2:8,9

No man works his way up to Heaven. Our eternal salvation is settled in the Saviour, not in the efforts of man.

"For there is one God, and one mediator between God and men, the man Christ Jesus."
I Timothy 2:5

We are saved by the grace of God through the crucifixion of Christ. Man must accept God's plan or prepare for His punishment.

"That if thou shalt confess with thy mouth the Lord Jesus, and shalt believe in thine heart that God hath raised him from the dead, thou shalt be saved."
Romans 10:9

The evidence of real Christian experience is a combination of what we feel in our hearts and what we say with our lives.

". . . The Lord is witness against you, and his anointed is witness this day . . ."
I Samuel 12:5

The testimony of a crucified Saviour will condemn or release one and all in the hour of judgment. Your future can be settled now by accepting Him.

"Behold, the Lord's hand is not shortened, that it cannot save; neither his ear heavy, that it cannot hear."

Isaiah 59:1

God is ever ready and ever merciful to hear the faintest cry and save the vilest sinner. "God is love."

———————

". . . behold, now is the accepted time; behold, now is the day of salvation."

II Corinthians 6:2

A man's life on earth and his eternal welfare in the life to come hinges on a decision that he can make in one minute. Decide now; your whole destiny depends on it.

———————

"Jesus answered and said unto him, Verily, verily, I say unto thee, Except a man be born again, he cannot see the kingdom of God."

John 3:3

It is impossible for man to have a new life without a new birth. Being a Christian is a great deal more than joining a church and making resolutions. It is experiencing a regeneration through a crucified Redeemer.

———————

"There is therefore now no condemnation to them which are in Christ Jesus, who walk not after the flesh, but after the Spirit."

Romans 8:1

The person who settles up with God here won't have to face an outstanding account in the life to come. "Believe on the Lord Jesus Christ, and thou shalt be saved."

———————

"But God commendeth his love toward us, in that, while we were yet sinners, Christ died for us."

Romans 5:8

Salvation is on a come-as-you-are basis, and people who consider themselves too good to be lost will never be saved. "All have sinned and come short of the glory of God."

———————

". . . him that cometh to me I will in no wise cast out."

John 6:37

Every honest seeker in Christ will find his eternal salvation. Nothing shall separate us from the love of God.

———————

"If we confess our sins, he is faithful and just to forgive us our sins, and to cleanse us from all unrighteousness."

I John 1:9

It is as we unburden ourselves to the Lord that He unveils His forgiveness to us. He said, "I will remember their iniquities no more." Believe it now, be happy forever.

––––––––

"And he said unto her, Thy sins are forgiven."

Luke 7:48

Man can excuse sin, but Jesus can forgive them. "If we confess our sins, he is faithful and just to forgive us our sins, and to cleanse us from all unrighteousness."

––––––––

"I, even I, am he that blotteth out thy transgressions for mine own sake, and will not remember thy sins."

Isaiah 43:25

God does what very few people attempt to do; forget the sins of others.

––––––––

"For all have sinned, and come short of the glory of God."

Romans 3:23

Even little sins can keep us from doing big things. Your Heavenly Father will forgive you for Christ's sake.

"Then they that gladly received his word were baptized: and the same day there were added unto them about three thousand souls. And they continued stedfastly in the apostles' doctrine and fellowship, and in breaking of bread, and in prayers."

Acts 2:41,42

After the revival, they were still around rejoicing and reaching out for others. This is the evidence of repentance and regeneration.

"And saying, The time is fulfilled, and the kingdom of God is at hand: repent ye, and believe the gospel."

Mark 1:15

Nothing happens in the heart until the mind is changed. "I thought on my ways, and turned my feet unto thy testimonies."

"Let the wicked forsake his way, and the unrighteous man his thoughts: and let him return unto the Lord, and he will have mercy upon him; and to our God, for he will abundantly pardon."
Isaiah 55:7

Here is the road back and the reason for taking it. "Seek ye the Lord while he may be found, call ye upon him while he is near." "There is forgiveness with thee." We praise thee, oh God.

———————

"If we confess our sins, he is faithful and just to forgive us our sins, and to cleanse us from all unrighteousness."
I John 1:9

We must acknowledge our need if we want it met. Pretence only prolongs the agony . . . and besides that, it is a frightening risk to take. "My Spirit will not always strive with man."

———————

"Come unto me, all ye that labour and are heavy laden, and I will give you rest. Take my yoke upon you, and learn of me; for I am meek and lowly in heart: and ye shall find rest unto your souls. For my yoke is easy, and my burden is light."

Matthew 11:28-30

You can't beat this invitation, but it's not going to be there forever. Today is the day of Salvation. You will never relive today. Make it a good one with God's help.

_____

"In the last day, that great day of the feast, Jesus stood and cried, saying, If any man thirst, let him come unto me, and drink."

John 7:37

Only Christ knows the real longing of every life, and He alone can fill it. Why wander in the wilderness ignoring His invitation? "Come unto me . . . I will give you rest."

_____

Serving God....

Serving God

"But ye are a chosen generation, a royal priesthood, an holy nation, a peculiar people; that ye should shew forth the praises of him who hath called you out of darkness into his marvellous light."

I Peter 2:9

We are not redeemed by God just to enjoy our experience, but to share it. He is not looking for authorities, just witnesses. "Let the redeemed of the Lord say so."

"I was glad when they said unto me, Let us go into the house of the Lord."

Psalms 122:1

You can tell those who love the Lord by the excuses they find to attend His House. You can also tell those who don't love Him so much by the excuses they seem to find to stay away from His House. Christ loved the Church, and gave Himself for it.

"Whatsoever thy hand findeth to do, do it with thy might; for there is no work, nor device, nor knowledge, nor wisdom, in the grave, whither thou goest."

Ecclesiastes 9:10

If more Christians would sincerely put their hands, hearts and heads in the work of the Lord, there would be such a change overnight that it would be hard for the world to recognize the Church.

"That if thou shalt confess with thy mouth the Lord Jesus, and shalt believe in thine heart that God hath raised him from the dead, thou shalt be saved."

Romans 10:9

The surrendered Christian life is a combination of believing, trusting and telling. "Trust in the Lord with all thine heart." "Go tell what great things the Lord hath done for thee."

"Only fear the Lord, and serve him in truth with all your heart: for consider how great things he hath done for you."

I Samuel 12:24

God calls for a great deal more than a part time commitment and a casual approach to Christianity. Seek Him with your whole heart and ye shall find Him.

"He must increase, but I must decrease."
John 3:30

The business of every Christian is to lift up the Saviour and play down self. The greatest problem of the Church is that we have not held Him up as the answer.

"I Jesus have sent mine angel to testify unto you these things in the churches. I am the root and the offspring of David, and the bright and morning star."

Revelation 22:16

Jesus still has a message for the Church today to be delivered by men who will tell it like it is, so that we may no longer be as we are. Preach the Word!

"Go ye therefore, and teach all nations, baptizing them in the name of the Father, and of the Son, and of the Holy Ghost: Teaching them to observe all things whatsoever I have commanded you: and, lo, I am with you alway, even unto the end of the world. Amen."

Matthew 28:19,20

The average church is designed to suit and seat the people, and all the while God intended it as an instrument to send us! On with the message of love . . . we have been seated long enough.

――――――――――

"Holding forth the word of life; that I may rejoice in the day of Christ, that I have not run in vain, neither laboured in vain."
Philippians 2:16

Here's news Christian friend. Our greatest job is not to explain the Word of God, but to extend it.

――――――――――

"Ye are the light of the world . . ."
Matthew 5:14

Not just the Church, not a select few, but each one in his own way that stands for the cause of Christianity. How much light have you been responsible for to dispense the gloom and doubt of a troubled soul yet in darkness?

――――――――――

"The night is far spent, the day is at hand: let us therefore cast off the works of darkness, and let us put on the armour of light."
Romans 13:12

The person who has the light ought to be shining. Let your light so shine that men may see your good works and glorify your Father, which is in Heaven.

"As thou hast sent me into the world, even so have I also sent them into the world."
John 17:18

The job of every Christian is to continue the work of Christ through personal experience and public example. "Ye are my witnesses."

"And he said unto them, Go ye into all the world, and preach the gospel to every creature."
Mark 16:15

As we are straining to reach the moon, we are faced with the mounting evidence to suggest that we haven't reached the earth as yet.

". . . Take heed to the ministry which thou hast received in the Lord, that thou fulfill it."

Colossians 4:17

God has big jobs that can be filled with little people. "He is no respector of persons."

———————

"But while men slept, his enemy came and sowed tares among the wheat, and went his way."

Matthew 13:25

Christians ought to be wide awake and up and doing. "The night cometh."

———————

"Remember now thy Creator in the days of thy youth . . ."

Ecclesiastes 12:1

You can't give God what's left of life and expect His best. Give Him the best and the rest of your life.

———————

"If ye love me, keep my commandments."
John 14:15

The need of the hour is for more Christians to obey the Lord's Word and do His work. A good test of our love for God is in how much we trust His Word.

"Behold, the Lord's hand is not shortened, that it cannot save; neither his ear heavy, that it cannot hear."

Isaiah 59:1

Wherever you are, He can hear you and reach you. Therefore, reach out and take the extended hand of Christ, and then be His instrument to touch a lost and dying world.

"Say not ye, There are yet four months, and then cometh harvest? behold, I say unto you, Lift up your eyes, and look on the fields; for they are white already to harvest."

John 4:35

The heart's cry of every Christian ought to be, "God give me a vision of what can be done and what must be done before it is too late." Work while it is day. The night cometh.

"For we cannot but speak the things which we have seen and heard."

Acts 4:20

If you find it difficult to speak for the Lord, consider the first Christians who said, "We can't help but speak." The need seems to be for more of what they had. "God is no respector of persons."

———————

"Ye are the salt of the earth: but if the salt have lost his savour, wherewith shall it be salted? it is thenceforth good for nothing, but to be cast out, and to be trodden under foot of men."

Matthew 5:13

There are too many tasteless Christians who could use a little spiritual seasoning to sharpen their testimony, and at the same time, help put a good taste in the mouth of the world they see daily.

———————

"Whosoever therefore shall confess me before men, him will I confess also before my Father which is in heaven."

Matthew 10:32

If you keep your salvation a secret here, don't expect such a royal reception in Heaven. "Ye are my witnesses."

"But the fruit of the Spirit is love, joy, peace, longsuffering, gentleness, goodness, faith, Meekness, temperance: against such there is no law."

Galatians 5:22,23

Not only the proclamation of Christianity, but the evidence of it, is important.

"For whom he did foreknow, he also did predestinate to be conformed to the image of his Son, that he might be the firstborn among many brethren."

Romans 8:29

If the world can catch the image of Christ in believers, it shouldn't be long in making the conversion. "Ye are my witnesses."

"Go ye therefore, and teach all nations, baptizing them in the name of the Father, and of the Son, and of the Holy Ghost: Teaching them to observe all things whatsoever I have commanded you: and, lo, I am with you alway, even unto the end of the world. Amen "

Matthew 28.19,20

You will be glad in eternity that you did all that you could to evangelize the earth. Do it with all your love, might and means.

"So likewise, whosoever he be of you that forsaketh not all that he hath, he cannot be my disciple '

Luke 14:33

God offers untold blessings for unconditional surrender. "Seek ye first the kingdom of God, and his righteousness; and all these things shall be added unto you "

"Take my yoke upon you, and learn of me; for I am meek and lowly in heart: and ye shall find rest unto your souls."

Matthew 11:29

The safest place and the sweetest place is to be in His will and at His service.

"And, behold, I come quickly; and my reward is with me, to give every man according as his work shall be."

Revelation 22:12

"When the roll is called up yonder" we will be rewarded in accordance with what we have done down here. Work while it is day. The night cometh when no man can work.

"For as the body without the spirit is dead, so faith without works is dead also."

James 2:26

The man who has faith ought to be anxious to prove that it is workable.

"Take ye heed, watch and pray: for ye know not when the time is."

Mark 13:33

Time is in God's hands; talents are in our hands. We ought to use them wisely before time runs out. "The time is short."

". . . who knoweth whether thou art come to the kingdom for such a time as this?"
Esther 4:14

God places us with a purpose, and He has never misplaced anyone.

"For we must all appear before the judgment seat of Christ; that every one may receive the things done in his body, according to that he hath done, whether it be good or bad."
II Corinthians 5:10

Every Christian will be judged as to how seriously he took the work of Christ and the worth of a soul. Have you given your best to Jesus?

". . . Thou shalt worship the Lord thy God, and him only shalt thou serve."

Matthew 4:10

Strange and curious gods daily make their appearance in all of our lives to crowd out the true and living God. Let it be known that you are not for hire. It is a noble thing to be a real servant.

"He that findeth his life shall lose it: and he that loseth his life for my sake shall find it."

Matthew 10:39

Man truly finds himself in life as he loses himself in the will of the Lord. Make the investment of thyself in the work of God; there are no greater dividends.

"And let us not be weary in well doing: for in due season we shall reap, if we faint not."

Galatians 6:9

The man who majors in doing good will not have bad memories.

"Therefore said he unto them, The harvest truly is great, but the labourers are few: pray ye therefore the Lord of the harvest, that he would send forth labourers into his harvest.''

Luke 10:2

We need more feeling for the field. "They are white already to harvest." It is important to work for the Lord, as well as worship Him.

''For whosoever will save his life shall lose it: but whosoever will lose his life for my sake, the same shall save it.''

Luke 9:24

There is no gift like the gift of thyself. The only thing that we save is what we give away. Lose yourself in the work of Christ here, and you will find yourself in Heaven.

''For whosoever shall give you a cup of water to drink in my name, because ye belong to Christ, verily I say unto you, he shall not lose his reward.''

Mark 9:41

Our attitude toward the little things are important.

"Withhold not good from them to whom it is due, when it is in the power of thine hand to do it."

Proverbs 3:27

If you are a Christian, the best thing that you can do for your neighbors is to introduce them to your best friend, Jesus. "He that winneth souls is wise."

———————

"And through thy knowledge shall the weak brother perish, for whom Christ died?"

I Corinthians 8:11

The man who helps another find his way is on the right track himself. "Let brotherly love continue."

———————

"That if thou shalt confess with thy mouth the Lord Jesus, and shalt believe in thine heart that God hath raised him from the dead, thou shalt be saved."

Romans 10:9

The Christian life ought to be full of believing, telling and sharing.

———————

"And he said unto them, Go ye into all the world, and preach the gospel to every creature. He that believeth and is baptized shall be saved; but he that believeth not shall be damned."

Mark 16:15,16

The Gospel is a subpoena, and every Christian is obligated to go out and serve it on a lost world. "Lo I am with you."

"My tongue also shall talk of thy righteousness all the day long . . ."

Psalms 71:24

Every Christian ought to have a testimony and not be ashamed to tell it.

"For we cannot but speak the things which we have seen and heard."

Acts 4:20

The man who has met the Lord is bound to tell of the meeting. "Let the redeemed of the Lord say so, whom he hath redeemed from the hand of the enemy."

". . . he that winneth souls is wise."
Proverbs 11:30

The best time that a man spends on earth is what he does in the interest of Heaven.

"And Jesus said unto them, Come ye after me, and I will make you to become fishers of men."

Mark 1:17

If it has not been your happy privilege to point a soul to Christ, it matters little else what your achievements have been. There is no business like God's business.

"For I have not shunned to declare unto you all the counsel of God."

Acts 20:27

The world has heard too much of the gospel according to man and too little of the Gospel according to God. Man is at his best when he is telling what the Lord has to say. "Preach the Word."

"Who gave himself for us, that he might redeem us from all iniquity, and purify unto himself a peculiar people, zealous of good works."

Titus 2:14

God is looking for bold and busy people to do big things."

". . . be thou faithful unto death, and I will give thee a crown of life."

Revelation 2:10

Be a career Christian.

". . . Here am I; send me."

Isaiah 6:8

The greatest contribution is the gift of ourselves in the service of the Lord. A lot of big jobs are waiting to be filled by dedicated little people.

"And they that be wise shall shine as the brightness of the firmament; and they that turn many to righteousness as the stars for ever and ever."

Daniel 12:3

Do something lasting and leave something lasting. Major in the main things of life; all else will vanish.

———————

". . . Lord, what wilt thou have me to do? And the Lord said unto him, Arise, and go into the city, and it shall be told thee what thou must do."

Acts 9:6

God will take the willing worker, all-out for Christ, in preference to the wise ones who feel they have all the answers.

———————

The Sovereignty of God....

The Sovereignty of God

"The earth is the Lord's, and the fulness thereof; the world, and they that dwell therein."
Psalms 24:1

Once the ownership is established, we shouldn't have any trouble with obedience. "Ye are not your own . . . " We have been purchased not with gold or silver, but by the precious blood of Christ.

"Hath not my hand made all these things?"
Acts 7:50

So little of our lives revolve around Him, who created us, and the world that we live in. So much depends on our attitude toward Him and what we do with the Saviour.

"Turn ye not unto idols, nor make to yourselves molten gods: I am the Lord your God."
Leviticus 19:4

Anything that is put ahead of God will be left behind. "Thou shalt worship the Lord thy God and him only shalt thou serve."

"For of him, and through him, and to him, are all things: to whom be glory for ever. Amen."
Romans 11:36

Life was made to revolve around God, and when it doesn't, we run into reverses.

"Ah Lord God! behold, thou hast made the heaven and the earth by thy great power and stretched out arm, and there is nothing too hard for thee."

Jeremiah 32:17

God can do anything, and without Him, we can do nothing.

"For by him were all things created, that are in heaven, and that are in earth, visible and invisible, whether they be thrones, or dominions, or principalities, or powers: all things were created by him, and for him: And he is before all things, and by him all things consist."

Colossians 1:16,17

God has a copyright on all creations. Man merely makes the discovery that after all is said and done, he belongs to Him.

"The earth is the Lord's, and the fulness thereof; the world, and they that dwell therein."
Psalms 24:1

This just about settles it for God. Happy is the man who recognizes who holds the whole world in the palm of His hand.

". . . they shall know that I am the Lord."
Ezekiel 28:23

God has a way of making Himself known and heard. "Seek ye the Lord while he may be found, call ye upon him while he is near."

"For as the heavens are higher than the earth, so are my ways higher than your ways, and my thoughts than your thoughts."
Isaiah 55:9

This does not mean that God is out of reach, but only that many times His reasoning is different than ours. Don't spend a lot of time trying to figure God out; just release your faith in humble obedience to His will and way.

"Known unto God are all his works from the beginning of the world."

Acts 15:18

Never mind if we can't figure everything out, so long as we know that our faithful Creator has everything in control. "Underneath are the everlasting arms." "Trust and obey."

"And the Lord said unto Moses, Rise up early in the morning, and stand before Pharaoh, and say unto him, Thus saith the Lord God of the Hebrews, Let my people go, that they may serve me. For I will at this time send all my plagues upon thine heart, and upon thy servants, and upon thy people; that thou mayest know that there is none like me in all the earth."

Exodus 9:13,14

The Lord has a way of getting the attention of those who are aggravating His people . . . and no one will doubt that He has spoken.

"Know ye not that ye are the temple of God, and that the Spirit of God dwelleth in you? If any man defile the temple of God, him shall God destroy; for the temple of God is holy, which temple ye are."

I Corinthians 3:16,17

Man is the property of God and He will not forever tolerate trespassing.

———————

"Now unto him that is able to do exceeding abundantly above all that we ask or think, according to the power that worketh in us."

Ephesians 3:20

No one can look at this and limit God. "For with God nothing shall be impossible." "I am the Lord, the God of all flesh . . . Is there anything too hard for me?"

———————

"Turn ye not unto idols, nor make to yourselves molten gods: I am the Lord your God."

Leviticus 19:4

Anything that is put ahead of God will be left behind. "Thou shalt worship the Lord thy God and Him only shalt thou serve."

Attend the services in your church and pray for God's servant. Blessings will be yours.

"O come, let us worship and bow down: let us kneel before the Lord our maker."
Psalms 95:6

Worship is more than sound. It is an act! It is a bowing of our wills and ways, a surrender to Him. We must not make the mistake of worshipping a cause, another Christian or even the Church. All the glory is due to God and must go to Him. Praise Him!

"Let all the earth fear the Lord: let all the inhabitants of the world stand in awe of him."
Psalms 33:8

We need but to look around us to know that there is a greater power above us. The need of the hour is for the created to have more respect for the Creator.

"Know ye that the Lord he is God: it is he that hath made us, and not we ourselves; we are his people and the sheep of his pasture."

Psalms 100:3

The strain of life and the sting of death are removed when we come to sit at the feet of the dear Shepherd. Jesus said, "I am the good shepherd: the good shepherd giveth his life for the sheep."

"Can any hide himself in secret places that I shall not see him? saith the Lord. Do not I fill heaven and earth? saith the Lord."

Jeremiah 23:24

God is everywhere, all powerful, and He loves you. Come out of your hiding, wherever you are, and open yourself up to His tender touch. Your Heavenly Father will forgive you. Whom the Son sets free is free indeed.

"I am the Lord: that is my name: and my glory will I not give to another, neither my praise to graven images."

Isaiah 42:8

Love and appreciate others and even love yourself, but all the glory and the praise, plus the greatest of our love must go to Him. All that we are, have, or will be is because of Him. "He hath made us and not we ourselves." Oh God, our Heavenly Father, we praise You and give honor and glory to Your name. Thank You for Jesus and the Holy Spirit and Your Word. We praise You for abundant life here and eternal life in Heaven, through Jesus Christ, Your Son. Amen.

"In that day shall the Lord defend the inhabitants of Jerusalem; and he that is feeble among them at that day shall be as David; and the house of David shall be as God, as the angel of the Lord before them."

Zechariah 12:8

With God, the weakest of vessels takes on the power and the authority of the Lord. 'I am with thee to deliver thee."

And the Lord shall be king over all the earth: in that day shall there be one Lord, and his name one."

Zechariah 14:9

The day will come when the One who made it all will rule over all. Blessed are those subjects who will already have made Him Lord of Lords and King of Kings.

"All the ends of the world shall remember and turn unto the Lord: and all the kindreds of the nations shall worship before thee. For the kingdom is the Lord's: and he is the governor among the nations."

Psalms 22:27,28

God has His way of bringing to pass what He has said. Woe to the people and nations that get in the way.

"Drop down, ye heavens, from above, and let the skies pour down righteousness: let the earth open, and let them bring forth salvation, and let righteousness spring up together; I the Lord have created it."

Isaiah 45:8

Listen to the Lord! A God who can speak with authority like that certainly has a good word for you. "Ask, and it shall be given you; seek, and ye shall find; knock, and it shall be opened unto you." Praise God.

"Be still, and know that I am God: I will be exalted among the heathen, I will be exalted in the earth."

Psalms 46:10

Some of the greatest victories that you will ever experience will not be in working for God, but in waiting on Him. Come out of your struggles and into His stillness and "know Him."

"And the God of peace shall bruise Satan under your feet shortly. The grace of our Lord Jesus Christ be with you. Amen."

Romans 16:20

Keep this in mind no matter how things look. God is in charge. Father, help us to recognize Your ability and our authority as believers. In Jesus' name. Amen.

"And Jesus looking upon them saith, With men it is impossible, but not with God: for with God all things are possible."

Mark 10:27

Nothing is out of reach as long as we can reach our Heavenly Father, and we can. Jesus said, "I am the way." Let's go with Him.

"Therefore let no man glory in men. For all things are yours."

I Cor. 3:21

Look at all we miss by not looking to God. "My God shall supply all of your need according to his riches in glory by Christ Jesus."

Spiritual Birth....

Spiritual Birth

"Therefore if any man be in Christ, he is a new creature: old things are passed away; behold, all things are become new."

II Corinthians 5:17

Our meeting with Christ always makes the difference. We will know it, and so will others. "Let your light so shine before men, that they may see your good works, and glorify your Father which is in heaven."

"There is therefore now no condemnation to them which are in Christ Jesus, who walk not after the flesh, but after the Spirit."

Romans 8:1

Regeneration in Christ brings release. Refuse to live in the past. "If any man be in Christ, he is a new creature: old things are passed away; behold, all things are become new."

"Jesus answered and said unto him, Verily, verily, I say unto thee, Except a man be born again, he cannot see the kingdom of God."

John 3:3

The new birth is a lot more than a decision to do a little better. It is a departure of

the old nature, giving way to new life in Christ.
It becomes "Christ in you the hope of glory."
Father, help us all to see how easy it is to
receive Jesus, and yet how easy it is to pass
Him by and lose eternal life forever.

". . . put off all these; anger, wrath, malice,
blasphemy, filthy communication out of your
mouth. Lie not one to another . . ."

Colossians 3:8,9

Here are some things that we can do
without in this life. When we put on the new
man through Christ, then we can put off the
old man with all his evil deeds.

"A new heart also will I give you, and a new
spirit will I put within you."

Ezekiel 36:26

You can't whitewash the old heart and
expect a new spirit. Allow God to make the
exchange of a lifetime, and give you a new
heart and a new spirit for a new year. "Old
things will pass away, and all things will
become new."

". . . Behold, I make all things new . . ."
Revelation 21:5

God has the power and is willing to give us a new start. If you are tired of the old life, then accept the new one that He has for you. "If any man be in Christ, he is a new creature: old things are passed away; behold, all things are become new."

———————

"Jesus answered and said unto him, Verily, verily, I say unto thee, Except a man be born again, he cannot see the kingdom of God."

John 3:3

Never have there been so many churches with the evidence of so few real Christians. It is highly possible for one to be known by everyone in church and yet be a stranger to Christ.

———————

"But the voice answered me again from heaven, What God hath cleansed, that call not thou common."

Acts 11:9

Whatever and whoever God touches is never the same. Regeneration elevates. "If any man be in Christ, he is a new creature:

old things are passed away, behold, all things are become new.''

———————————

"Jesus answered and said unto him, Verily, verily, I say unto thee, Except a man be born again, he cannot see the kingdom of God.''
John 3:3

What the world needs is not only born leaders, but born-again leaders. You can be born again. "Ye must be born again.''

———————————

"Jesus answered and said unto him, Verily, verily, I say unto thee, Except a man be born again, he cannot see the kingdom of God.''
John 3:3

What good would it do to refine man if he is not regenerated? The heart of man, as well as the head of man, must be reached. Culture may polish up a man, but only Christ can really cleanse him.

———————————

"Come now, and let us reason together, saith the Lord: though your sins be as scarlet, they shall be as white as snow; though they be red like crimson, they shall be as wool."

Isaiah 1:18

If an artist is able to take a piece of junk and make it into a thing of beauty, think of what the Lord can do with our lives turned over to Him. Let the Lord Redeemer recycle your life today. You will be glad with the results.

"Jesus answered and said unto him, Verily, verily, I say unto thee, Except a man be born again, he cannot see the kingdom of God."

John 3:3

Do you know the process? Simply pray, Father, I receive Jesus as my Saviour on the basis that He died for my sins, and that I cannot be saved without Him. I repent of my sins, and I release it all to You. In Jesus' name. Amen. Thank You.

"That which is born of the flesh is flesh; and that which is born of the Spirit is spirit."

John 3:6

Here is the heart of God in the interest of the souls of men. The next move is yours. Jesus said, "Come unto me . . . him that cometh to me I will in no wise cast out."

———————

"Jesus answered and said unto him, Verily, verily, I say unto thee, Except a man be born again, he cannot see the kingdom of God."

John 3:3

This is more than a term. It is an experience, without which, we are not ready to meet God. It means being born from above, and it can happen right now by praying a prayer like this. Father, I repent of my sins, and I receive the Lord Jesus, Your Son, into my heart as my personal Savior and Lord of my life. Amen.

———————

"Enter ye in at the strait gate: for wide is the gate, and broad is the way, that leadeth to destruction, and many there be which go in threat: Because strait is the gate, and narrow is the way, which leadeth unto life, and few there be that find it."

Matthew 7:13,14

Heaven is no walk-in or pushover. "Except a man be born again, he cannot see the kingdom of God."

"Now unto him that is able to keep you from falling, and to present you faultless before the presence of his glory with exceeding joy."

Jude 24

Don't worry about the carry-over of the old life once you have surrendered it to Him. "If any man be in Christ, he is a new creature." "Behold, I make all things new."

"For the Lord himself shall descend from heaven with a shout, with the voice of the archangel, and with the trump of God: and the dead in Christ shall rise first: Then we which are alive and remain shall be caught up together with them in the clouds to meet the Lord in the air: and so shall we ever be with the Lord.''

I Thessalonians 4:16,17

What a beautiful picture of the future! But remember, there is no reunion without regeneration! "Except a man be born again, he cannot see the kingdom of God." You can take care of that in the next moment by turning from your sins and inviting Jesus into your heart.

———————

Spiritual Neglect....

Spiritual Neglect

"Nevertheless I have some what against thee, because thou hast left thy first love."

Revelation 2:4

The Lord's message to the Church is simply to "come back" from our wanderings, get off the religious routine bit, and get on with the message that man is a sinner and Jesus is the Saviour, and without Him there is no redemption. Only in this is there hope for the Church and help for the world.

"Because that, when they knew God, they glorified him not as God, neither were thankful; but became vain in their imaginations, and their foolish heart was darkened. Professing themselves to be wise, they became fools."

Romans 1:21,22

The road to decay is often marked by signs of deceit, ingratitude, self esteem and God rejection.

"And Peter remembered the word of Jesus, which said unto him, Before the cock crow, thou shalt deny me thrice. And he went out, and wept bitterly."

Matthew 26:75

Tears have been the way back for many discouraged Christians who have warmed themselves by the enemy's fire. He will not turn thee away.

"Nevertheless I have some what against thee, because thou hast left thy first love."
Revelation 2:4

It is a costly thing to allow cares and circumstances to crowd Christ out of your life. "Return ye."

"Stand fast therefore in the liberty wherewith Christ hath made us free, and be not entangled again with the yoke of bondage."
Galatians 5:1

We must enjoy and exercise the freedom that Christ has given us, or become subject to the former things that bound us.

"He that hath no rule over his own spirit is like a city that is broken down, and without walls."

Proverbs 25:28

It is so easy to lose control if Christ is not at the center of your life. "Let the Spirit of Christ reign in your heart."

"And because iniquity shall abound, the love of many shall wax cold."

Matthew 24:12

One of the great signs of the times is the priority given to sin. "As it was in the days of Noah, so shall it be also in the days of the coming of the Son of Man."

"For the love of money is the root of all evil: which while some coveted after, they have erred from the faith, and pierced themselves through with many sorrows."

I Timothy 6:10

If you are inclined to be impressed by those who appear to have it made, take another look at what it has made of them. "Seek ye first the kingdom of God, and his righteousness; and all these things shall be added unto you."

———————————

"For if after they have escaped the pollutions of the world through the knowledge of the Lord and Saviour Jesus Christ, they are again entangled therein, and overcome, the latter end is worse with them than the beginning."

II Peter 2:20

In a world of pollution talk, it makes good sense for us to hear what the Lord has to say about the future a man has who cleans the air regarding his spiritual experience, and then sets out on a "do it yourself" plan. Beware, lest we ignore the pitfalls and disregard the power of Him who is able to keep us. Remember, the Lord, Jesus said, "Without me ye can do nothing" . . . but we are more than conquerors through Him that loved us.

———————————

"Stand fast therefore in the liberty where with Christ hath made us free, and be not entangled again with yoke of bondage."

Galatians 5:1

Most of our fears are of our own making, because we have not made Him Master and Lord of our life. "Perfect love casteth out fear." "Fear thou not for I am with thee . . ."

———————

"And the people said unto Joshua, Nay; but we will serve the lord."

Joshua 24:21

How many of us have made the same commitment to the Lord, only to lose it in a shuffle of simple things we regarded as important? This week, take your family back to the House of God and get the same good feeling that only a renewal of your faith can bring. You need your church and your church needs you.

———————

"They soon forgat his works; they waited not for his counsel . . . And he gave them their request; but sent leanness into their soul."

Psalms 106:13,15

Many a person has discovered that what they begged God for satisfied the flesh for a season, but it starved the soul. "Seek ye first the kingdom of God, and his righteousness; and all these things shall be added unto you."

"And Moses went up unto God, and the Lord called unto him out of the mountain, saying, Thus shalt thou say to the house of Jacob, and tell the children of Israel . . . Now therefore, if ye will obey my voice indeed, and keep my covenant, then ye shall be a peculiar treasure unto me above all people: for all the earth is mine."

Exodus 19:3,5

If the fulfillment of His promises seem to elude us, it could be that we have failed to obey the conditions.

"Now therefore stand still, that I may reason with you before the Lord of all the righteous acts of the Lord, which he did to you and your fathers."

I Samuel 12:7

In a fast moving world, there is a great danger of forgetting where we are going and where we started. Stand still and see the salvation of the Lord.

". . . Today if ye will hear his voice, harden not your hearts . . ."

Hebrews 3:15

The man who ignores the voice of God runs the risk of never hearing it again. "My Spirit will not always strive with man . . ."

"And the Lord said, My Spirit shall not always strive with man . . ."

Genesis 6:3

Pity the person who, through his own neglect, puts himself out of the reach of God. The Lord has sent the Holy Spirit to bring you in. Don't turn Him away.

"Neglect not the gift that is in thee . . ."
I Timothy 4:14

We need to develop our own God-given talents, instead of trying to duplicate what He has given to another.

"How shall we escape, if we neglect so great salvation . . ."

Hebrews 2:3

Put-off and put-on are two of man's greatest enemies. Give God your answer to-day to this great question. "My Spirit will not always strive with man."

"And Jesus said unto him, No man, having put his hand to the plough, and looking back, is fit for the kingdom of God."

Luke 9:62

More Christians are needed with the forward look. Too much time is spent at the tombstones of past experiences.

"I will heal their backsliding, I will love them freely; for mine anger is turned away from him."

Hosea 14:4

Every man knows where he is with God, but nothing happens until he turns around. "I thought on my ways and I turned." "Except ye repent, ye shall all likewise perish."

———————

Trusting God....

Trusting God

"Blessed be the Lord, that hath given rest unto his people Israel, according to all that he promised: there hath not failed one word of all his good promise, which he promised by the hand of Moses his servant."

I Kings 8:56

Look at the record and leave the rest to Him. He will keep His Word with you. We are but to claim it.

———————

"And Joseph said unto them, Fear not: for am I in the place of God? But as for you, ye thought evil against me; but God meant it unto good, to bring to pass, as it is this day, to save much people alive."

Genesis 50:19,20

God has a way of taking what seems to be a big mistake and making a great miracle out of it. As for us, we are inclined to get disappointments and appointments mixed up. Walk away from your problem and let God work on the answer. When you see what He comes up with, you will be glad you didn't try to work it out.

———————

"That thy trust may be in the Lord, I have made known to thee this day, even to thee. Have not I written to thee excellent things in counsels and knowledge.''

Proverbs 22:19,20

Life's answers are lost to us because we keep leaning on our own understanding or taking the advice of those who are as much in the dark as we are. Read the Bible every day and apply it to your everyday need.

". . . thou hast made the heaven and the earth by thy great power . . . and there is nothing too hard for thee.''

Jeremiah 32:17

If He can make the heaven and the earth, you surely can trust Him with your problem. Believe that. He is great enough and willing to meet your every need. "All power is given unto me in Heaven and in earth.''

"Trust ye in the Lord for ever: for in the Lord JEHOVAH is everlasting strength."

Isaiah 26:4

Enlist your life in the service of the Lord forever. Don't worry about the "holding out", for in Him is "everlasting strength." "I will uphold thee with the right hand of my righteousness." "Have faith in God."

"But without faith it is impossible to please him: for he that cometh to God must believe that he is, and that he is a rewarder of them that diligently seek him."

Hebrews 11:6

Nothing that we can do for God can ever take the place of our trust in Him. It is altogether possible to be a tireless worker for the Lord and, yet, to be timid in our trust.

"Unto thee, O Lord, do I lift up my soul . . . I trust in thee . . ."

Psalms 25:1,2

The man who lifts the burdens of life to God in sincerity will never be let down. "He careth for you."

"Thus saith the Lord, thy Redeemer, the Holy One of Israel; I am the Lord thy God which teacheth thee to profit, which leadeth thee by the way that thou shouldest go."

Isaiah 48:17

Don't hesitate to ask God for guidance. Don't question the way He leads. He will guide you into all truth.

———————

"But it is good for me to draw near to God: I have put my trust in the Lord God, that I may declare all thy works."

Psalms 73:28

Our greatest need is to be near to God. All else that is good and worthwhile will follow. "Draw nigh to God, and he will draw nigh to you."

———————

"And Jesus looking upon them saith, With men it is impossible, but not with God: for with God all things are possible."

Mark 10:27

You have tried everything else, why not try God? He is able to do and undo, and is limited only by what we will believe Him for. "I am the Lord, I change not."

———————

"And it is easier for heaven and earth to pass, than one tittle of the law to fail."

Luke 16:17

The Lord has never been known to go back on His Word or back down on His promises. "Only believe."

———————

"What time I am afraid, I will trust in thee."

Psalms 56:3

If fear overtakes you, hurry to your Heavenly Father. He loves you and has the answer for every problem.

———————

"My covenant will I not break, nor alter the thing that is gone out of my lips."

Psalms 89:34

In an age of broken promises, God stands ready to keep His Word with the humblest believer.

"What time I am afraid, I will trust in thee."
Psalms 56:3

When we treat fear with trust, all the terrors of life must go. "I will never leave thee nor forsake thee."

"Behold, I will do a new thing; now it shall spring forth; shall ye not know it? I will even make a way in the wilderness, and rivers in the desert."
Isaiah 43:19

We serve a creative God whose power adjusts to every problem of life. He will walk you through your wilderness, making a way where there is no way. Trust Him.

TRUSTING GOD

"And the Lord shall help them, and deliver them: he shall deliver them from the wicked, and save them, because they trust in him."

Psalms 37:40

The Lord is in the deliverance business. Special delivery! "Behold, I am the Lord, the God of all flesh: is there anything too hard for me?"

———————————

Words of
Warning....

Words of Warning

"For what shall it profit a man, if he shall gain the whole world, and lose his own soul? Or what shall a man give in exchange for his soul?"
Mark 8:36,37

An eternity without God and the good things He has prepared is a terrible price to pay for having our own way over things that will soon pass away. "Seek ye first the kingdom of God, and his righteousness; and all these things shall be added unto you."

". . . and God is angry with the wicked every day."

Psalms 7:11

He is a God of love, compassion, and longsuffering, but He is also a God of judgment. You cannot forever trample under foot the Word of God, the stern commandments of God, reject His Son, and go unpunished.

"Therefore be ye also ready: for in such an hour as ye think not the Son of man cometh."
Matthew 24:44

A person who is not ready to die is not ready to live. A person who is not ready to meet his Master in His second coming cannot fully appreciate the fact that He came the first time.

"Thou shalt not take the name of the Lord thy God in vain . . ."

Deuteronomy 5:11

Think on the holiness of God. Dwell on the power He has over the world and you, and let the mind of the Master be the master of your mind. Remember, "His ear is not heavy that it cannot hear."

". . . it is appointed unto men once to die, but after this the judgment."

Hebrews 9:27

That we must appear to account for the way we have lived this life is a truth that we must all face. How we live and how we die will determine our eternal future.

"Ye shall seek me, and shall not find me
. . ."

John 7:34

Man pays a terrible price for his pride.
"Today if ye will hear his voice, harden not
your hearts."

"And, behold, I come quickly; and my
reward is with me, to give every man according
as his work shall be."

Revelation 22:12

The world's greatest surprise may be
at our doorstep. He has not said in vain, "I
shall come again." Even so, come Lord
Jesus.

"But they made light of it . . ."

Matthew 22:5

Humanity has ever been the same. The
seriousness of the invitation did not register
with them then, and the majority of our day
do not see the tragedy of their refusal in accepting the Saviour. Decide now. A man may
be almost saved, yet entirely lost. Don't make

light of the invitation. Eternity is a long time to remember that you rejected it.

"For what is a man profited, if he shall gain the whole world, and lose his own soul? or what shall a man give in exchange for his soul?"
Matthew 16:26

Nothing on earth is worth keeping you out of Heaven. Count the cost!

"Beware that thou forget not the Lord thy God, in not keeping his commandments, and his judgments, and his statutes, which I command thee this day."
Deuteronomy 8:11

The man or the nation who forgets God will be reminded. Keep God in mind and His work at heart.

"I tell you, in that night there shall be two men in one bed; the one shall be taken, and the other shall be left. Two women shall be grinding together; the one shall be taken, and the other left."

Luke 17:34,35

Will you be among the missing or the misinformed? Read your Bible. Jesus said, "I will come again."

———

". . . Yet a little while am I with you, and then I go unto him that sent me. Ye shall seek me, and shall not find me: and where I am, thither ye cannot come."

John 7:33,34

Jesus is saying: "Some day you will want me and I will not be available". "My Spirit will not always strive with man". "Seek ye the Lord while he may be found, call ye upon him while he is near".

———

"Who fed thee in the wilderness with manna, which thy fathers knew not, that he might humble thee, and that he might prove thee, to do thee good at thy latter end."

Deuteronomy 8:16

If you have moved on to bigger things, as you see it, you would be wise to remember who took care of you in the wilderness. Otherwise, you may have another look at it!

"Then said he unto them, Nation shall rise against nation, and kingdom against kingdom: And great earthquakes shall be in divers places, and famines, and pestilences; and fearful sights and great signs shall there be from heaven."

Luke 21:10,11

More signs that His coming could be soon. When you read the Bible today, you would think that it was written yesterday. Jesus said, "In such an hour as ye think not, the Son of man cometh."

"For thou shalt worship no other god: for the Lord, whose name is Jealous, is a jealous God."

Exodus 34:14

Look out for the little gods. They have a way of growing, and no matter how small, they can separate us from the true and living God.

"Beware that thou forget not the Lord thy God, in not keeping his commandments, and his judgments, and his statutes, which I command thee this day."

Deuteronomy 8:11

Don't forget to remember from whence you came, and who has brought you to where you are, and where you are going.

"I tell you, in that night there shall be two men in one bed; the one shall be taken, and the other shall be left. Two women shall be grinding together; the one shall be taken, and the other left. Two men shall be in the field; the one shall be taken, and the other left. And they answered and said unto him, Where, Lord? And he said unto them, Wheresoever the body is, thither will the eagles be gathered together."

Luke 17:34-37

Here is a picture of the final day on earth of people who will probably have plans of what all they are going to do for the Lord, and others who were going to get right with the Lord. Do it now. "No man knoweth the day nor the hour when the Son of man cometh."

". . . there shall be a resurrection of the dead, both of the just and unjust."

Acts 24:15

Make no mistake about it. We all must appear before our Maker. You may have all the answers now, but how will it be when you stand before Him? Live today as though tomorrow you would face Him.

———————

". . . how is it that ye do not discern this time?"

Luke 12:56

If we fail to heed the signs, we will soon lose our way. These are days of signs and wonders, the greatest wonder being that we fail to see it.

———————

"Which also said, Ye men of Galilee, why stand ye gazing up into heaven? this same Jesus, which is taken up from you into heaven, shall so come in like manner as ye have seen him go into heaven."

Acts 1:11

The greatest surprise this world has ever known could be just around the corner. "In such an hour as ye think not, the Son of man cometh." Jesus said, "I will come again."

"But he that knew not, and did commit things worthy of stripes, shall be beaten with few stripes. For unto whomsoever much is given, of him shall be much required: and to whom men have committed much, of him they will ask the more."

Luke 12:48

God will require of nations and individuals a final accounting of what we did with what He gave us.

"For God so loved the world, that he gave his only begotten Son, that whosoever believeth

in him should not perish, but have everlasting
life.''

John 3:16

Here in the Word of God is the world's
greatest news coupled with the saddest
news. The future of every person is dependent on whether he ignores it or embraces it.

''I will therefore put you in remembrance,
though ye once knew this, how that the Lord, having saved the people out of the land of Egypt,
afterward destroyed them that believed not.''

Jude 5

Don't presume on the patience and
longsuffering of the Lord. ''My Spirit will not
always strive with man.''

"Knowing this first, that there shall come in the last days scoffers, walking after their own lusts, And saying, Where is the promise of his coming? for since the fathers fell asleep, all things continue as they were from the beginning of the creation."

II Peter 3:3,4

This is the day of the vocal unbelievers. The day of victory and vengeance of the Lord cannot be far away. Behold, He cometh. When ye shall see these things come to pass, look up.

———————

"And whosoever was not found written in the book of life was cast into the lake of fire."
Revelation 20:15

For the man who is trying to make a name here, it is good to give some serious thought as to where it will appear in the life to come.

———————

"Blow ye the trumpet in Zion, and sound an alarm in my holy mountain: let all the inhabitants of the land tremble: for the day of the Lord cometh, for it is nigh at hand."
Joel 2:1

It is the responsibility of every believer to sound the alarm. It is up to every man, on his own, to get up and answer the call. Don't turn the alarm off and go back to sleep, or let it run down. "My Spirit will not always strive with man."

"Therefore thus will I do unto thee, O Israel: and because I will do this unto thee, prepare to meet thy God, O Israel."

Amos 4:12

The most sobering thought in this life is that in the next we must account to Him who has made it. Where will you spend eternity? How are you spending life here?

"Be not deceived; God is not mocked: for whatsoever a man soweth, that shall he also reap."

Galatians 6:7

A person has to be careful of the seed that he sows. The day of harvest will come.

"And if any man shall take away from the words of the book of this prophecy, God shall take away his part out of the book of life, and out of the holy city, and from the things which are written in this book."

Revelation 22:19

People who alter the Word to their liking will have to give an account to the Lord.

———————

"And I saw the dead, small and great, stand before God; and the books were opened: and another book was opened, which is the book of life: and the dead were judged out of those things which were written in the books, according to their works."

Revelation 20:12

Never forget that we are judged by our works, but saved by His grace; and we must accept Him as Saviour or face Him as Judge.

———————

"And the Lord hath done to him, as he spake by me: for the Lord hath rent the kingdom out of thine hand, and given it to thy neighbour, even to David: Because thou obeyedst not the voice of the Lord, nor executedst his fierce wrath upon

Amalek, therefore hath the Lord done this thing unto thee this day.''

I Samuel 28:17,18

Any time we get too busy to listen or too big to obey, the Lord always has someone waiting to take our place.

''I will lay thy cities waste, and thou shalt be desolate, and thou shalt know that I am the Lord. Because thou hast had a perpetual hatred, and hast shed the blood of the children of Israel by the force of the sword in the time of their calamity, in the time that their iniquity had an end.''

Ezekiel 35:4,5

All mankind must remember that God cannot be pushed too far. He who is capable of great love is also capable of sure punishment.

"Thus they provoked him to anger with their inventions: and the plague brake in upon them."
Psalms 106:29

Perhaps we have yet to see the final cost of many of our achievements and the misuse of the great knowledge that God has entrusted to us.

———————

"And in hell he lift up his eyes, being in torments, and seeth Abraham afar off, and Lazarus in his bosom."
Luke 16:23

One minute after you have missed Heaven, you will know that hell is no myth. The only way out is in Him. "Believe on the Lord Jesus Christ and thou shalt be saved."

———————

"Thou shalt not take the name of the Lord thy God in vain; for the Lord will not hold him guiltless that taketh his name in vain."
Exodus 20:7

God is not taking lightly the language used involving His name and bringing reproach to His cause.

———————

"Can thine heart endure, or can thine hands be strong, in the days that I shall deal with thee? I the Lord have spoken it, and will do it."

Ezekiel 22:14

The judgment of God is no joke! Any nation or anyone who backs themselves into a corner, through open rebellion and unbelief, has good cause to be concerned. Jesus said, "Except ye repent, ye shall all likewise perish."

———————

"Watch therefore, for ye know neither the day nor the hour wherein the Son of man cometh."

Matthew 25:13

We are told not to set the time, but to make use of what we have left. In such an hour as ye think not, the Son of Man cometh. "Even so, come Lord Jesus."

———————

"For nation shall rise against nation, and kingdom against kingdom: and there shall be earthquakes in divers places, and there shall be famines and troubles: these are the beginnings of sorrows."

Mark 13:8

If you have missed the news, catch it in the Bible. You will probably be out in front! Thy Word is truth.

———————

"Take ye heed, watch and pray: for ye know not when the time is."

Mark 13:33

Time is in God's hands. Talents are in our hands. We ought to use them wisely before time runs out. The time is short.

———————

"The earth also was corrupt before God, and the earth was filled with violence . . . And God said unto Noah, The end of all flesh is come before me; for the earth is filled with violence through them; and, behold, I will destroy them with the earth."

Genesis 6:11,13

God warns from the past what we can expect in the future. What they saw in the beginning, we are experiencing in the present. But look up and get ready. As it was in the days of Noah, so shall it be also in the days of the coming of the Son of Man.

"Be ye therefore ready also: for the Son of man cometh at an hour when ye think not."
Luke 12:40

When we least expect Him, Jesus Christ, unannounced, will come back to take away every believer. If it happened tonight, where would you be tomorrow?

"The eyes of the Lord are in every place, beholding the evil and the good."
Proverbs 15:3

The Lord sees everything and knows every thought. No evil thing will go unnoticed. No good thing will go unrewarded.

". . . if that servant say in his heart, My lord delayeth his coming . . . The lord of that servant will come in a day when he looketh not for him, and at an hour when he is not aware, and will cut him in sunder, and will appoint him his portion with the unbelievers."

Luke 12:45,46

The second coming of Christ will be swift and sure, full of shocks and surprises. Perhaps some of the most surprised will be His servants.

———————

"He that believeth on the Son hath everlasting life: and he that believeth not the Son shall not see life; but the wrath of God abideth on him."

John 3:36

Here is what Jesus had to say about man's future. Everything that really counts is riding on what we do with Christ.

———————

". . . there shall be weeping and gnashing of teeth."

Matthew 24:51

This is how Jesus described a future without God and apart from Heaven. "Choose you this day whom ye will serve."

"Seek ye the Lord while he may be found, call ye upon him while he is near."

Isaiah 55:6

The risk of tomorrow is too great to ignore the important issues of today. This is your day.

"Ye shall seek me, and shall not find me . . ."

John 7:34

The worst thing that can happen to a man is not for his prayers to go unanswered, but for his prayers not to be heard.

"And why stand we in jeopardy every hour?"

I Corinthians 15:30

The person who won't stand up for Christ here won't stand a chance in Heaven. It is a risky thing to live in this world and ignore its Creator.

"And as it is appointed unto men once to die, but after this the judgment."

Hebrews 9:27

The most sobering thought of life is that after it is all over, we must give an account of every minute of it.

"For the wages of sin is death; but the gift of God is eternal life through Jesus Christ our Lord."

Romans 6:23

Everyone is paid by the master he serves. Life here is full of pay-backs. Eternity is full of play-backs with no take-backs.

Miscellany....

Miscellany

"For God so loved the world, that he gave his only begotten Son, that whosoever believeth in him should not perish, but have everlasting life."

John 3:16

This is Jesus telling what it took to bring mankind back to his Maker. To accept Him is life eternal. To reject Him is separation forever. Could this be your favorite verse which you have often quoted, but never experienced?

"And now I am no more in the world, but these are in the world, and I come to thee. Holy Father, keep through thine own name those whom thou hast given me, that they may be one, as we are."

John 17:11

The greatest need of the Church today is to have an old-fashioned family reunion with Jesus at the head of the table!

"So shall my word be that goeth forth out of my mouth: it shall not return unto me void, but it shall accomplish that which I please, and it shall prosper in the thing whereto I sent it."

Isaiah 55:11

If we want to be a part of a sure producer, we need to make sure that we are projecting His Word. Remember, it's His Word, not ours, that He has promised to bless.

"But if from thence thou shalt seek the Lord thy God, thou shalt find him, if thou seek him with all thy heart and with all thy soul."

Deuteronomy 4:29

Whoever you are, and wherever you are along the road of life, if you get serious with God, you are going to see things you never dreamed possible. "Seek ye the Lord while he may be found . . . call ye upon him while he is near."

"I am the vine, ye are the branches: He that abideth in me, and I in him, the same bringeth forth much fruit: for without me ye can do nothing."

John 15:5

Abiding in Him is even more productive than activity for Him. "Not by might, nor by power, but by my spirit, saith the Lord."

"For Christ sent me not to baptize, but to preach the gospel: not with wisdom of words, lest the cross of Christ should be made of none effect. For the preaching of the cross is to them that perish foolishness; but unto us which are saved it is the power of God."

1 Corinthians 1:17,18

The cross is where the sins of the whole world were paid for . . . but every person must acknowledge it was for him, before he can be pardoned. A simple prayer will see you through. Father, I admit my sins. I acknowledge Jesus as the One who died for them. I receive Him now as my Saviour. In His name. Amen.

_____

"Let the words of my mouth, and the meditation of my heart, be acceptable in thy sight, O Lord, my strength, and my redeemer."

Psalms 19:14

Not only what we talk about, but what we think about, is screened by the Lord. Is it acceptable to the Lord?

_____

"And when forty years were expired, there appeared to him in the wilderness of mount Sina an angel of the Lord in a flame of fire in a bush."

Acts 7:30

God is still speaking through unusual means, and many times through unknown people, to get His message across.

"Verily, verily, I say unto you, He that believeth on me, the works that I do shall he do also; and greater works than these shall he do; because I go unto my Father. And whatsoever ye shall ask in my name, that will I do, that the Father may be glorified in the Son. If ye shall ask any thing in my name, I will do it."

John 14:12-14

Release your faith with me, as we look to the Father. Jesus, I take You at Your Word and believe now that multitudes will be saved, believers filled with the Holy Spirit, others healed, and needs met in every part of their lives, in Your name and for the glory of God. Amen.

"For the wages of sin is death; but the gift of God is eternal life through Jesus Christ our Lord."

Romans 6:23

Every day, the average man neglects and forsakes the Greatest Gift in his mad and desperate search for worldly goods.

"And God hath set some in the church, first apostles, secondarily prophets, thirdly teachers, after that miracles, then gifts of healings, helps, governments, diversities of tongues."

I Corinthians 12:28

The average church is without New Testament excitement, because we have regarded ourselves as engineers of a program, rather than instruments through which the Holy Spirit can demonstrate His power.

"And the Lord said unto Joshua, See, I have given into thine hand Jericho, and the king thereof, and the mighty men of valour . . . and they took the city."

Joshua 6:2,20

The Bible is full of stories about ordinary people who went to war armed with nothing but the Word of God and won. "The grass withereth, the flower fadeth: but the word of our God shall stand forever."

"For where two or three are gathered together in my name, there am I in the midst of them."

Matthew 18:20

Careful that you don't make light of a few believers gathered, unless you want to take the responsibility of counting the presence of the Saviour as nothing.

"Behold, the Lord's hand is not shortened, that it cannot save; neither his ear heavy, that it cannot hear."

Isaiah 59:1

God has a strong arm, a ready ear, and a compassionate heart . . . and He loves you. Right now you can get right with Him. Father, in the next moment, help the readers to take care of all eternity by receiving Jesus into their hearts. Amen.

"But thanks be to God, which giveth us the victory through our Lord Jesus Christ."

I Corinthians 15:57

How true it is militarily or spiritually, there is no substitute for victory. Don't settle for a stand-off. "We are more than conquerors through him that loved us."

"And the work of righteousness shall be peace; and the effect of righteousness quietness and assurance for ever."

Isaiah 32:17

When we see the good that righteous living offers here and in the hereafter, can we really consider anything else? "The way of transgressors is hard." "Righteousness exalteth a nation: but sin is a reproach to any people."

"For I delivered unto you first of all that which I also received, how that Christ died for our sins according to the scriptures."

I Corinthians 15:3

The shame of our Christian experience is that we have missed the magnitude of the cross. Daily, we need to remember that He

died in our place, for our sins, and that our
pardon is only in believing it and receiving
Him.

"Thou art my hiding place; thou shalt
preserve me from trouble; thou shalt compass me
about with songs of deliverance. Selah."

Psalms 32:7

The only security that will stand up is
in the shelter of His arms. Come out, come
out, wherever you are, from your own hiding
place of fear and fright into the haven of rest
provided in the resurrected Christ, and go
free forever.

"The heart is deceitful above all things, and
desperately wicked . . ."

Jeremiah 17:9

The heart is what we are and where we
live. It remains so until it is renovated and
made ready for the Redeemer to move in.
Give Him His rightful place in your heart.

"He giveth power to the faint: and to them that have no might he increaseth strength."
Isaiah 40:29

The Christian's true strength is realized only in his whole-hearted surrender. The way out is up.

"And he that reapeth receiveth wages, and gathereth fruit unto life eternal: that both he that soweth and he that reapeth may rejoice together."
John 4:36

Life is a matter of sowing and reaping. Be careful what you sow; the harvest will come with rejoicing or with regrets.

"And they went forth, and preached every where, the Lord working with them, and confirming the word with signs following. Amen."
Mark 16:20

The Christian life should be full of signs and wonders.

"But thanks be to God, which giveth us the victory through our Lord Jesus Christ."
I Corinthians 15:57

There is a victory in the valley with Him who gives us a passing gear and a rising gear. The Lord takes the pressure and struggle out of religion, and lets us know that there are good times in God's service. Too many of us are content in holding on to what we have, at the cost of overlooking what God has for us.

"For whosoever shall do the will of God, the same is my brother, and my sister, and mother."

Mark 3:35

The people close to Christ will be those who have chosen His will above theirs. "Thy will be done."

"And whosoever of you will be the chiefest, shall be servant of all."

Mark 10:44

Not many people are aspiring to the great position of a true servant to mankind and our Maker. Most of us become slaves to goals without God.

"But my God shall supply all your need according to his riches in glory by Christ Jesus."
Philippians 4:19

Things will come a great deal easier in life, once we get our eyes off earthly circumstances and catch a glimpse of the Heavenly supply. "All that I have is thine."

"For by thee I have run through a troop; and by my God have I leaped over a wall."
Psalms 18:29

Don't worry about the walls if you are moving in His Divine will. March against them in His name, and they will fall.

"Go to the ant, thou sluggard; consider her ways, and be wise."
Proverbs 6:6

God has placed a lot of little things on earth to teach us big lessons.

"Come unto me, all ye that labour and are heavy laden, and I will give you rest. Take my yoke upon you, and learn of me; for I am meek and lowly in heart: and ye shall find rest unto your souls. For my yoke is easy, and my burden is light.''

Matthew 11:28-30

There is no rest and assurance, until we stop and surrender our all to the Almighty.

———————

''For what is a man profited, if he shall gain the whole world, and lose his own soul? or what shall a man give in exchange for his soul?''

Matthew 16:26

Neither the believer nor the unbeliever would ever need any prompting, if, for just once, we could catch a glimpse of the value of one soul.

———————

''And God saw that the wickedness of man was great in the earth, and that every imagination of the thoughts of his heart was only evil continually.''

Genesis 6:5

This was God's observation at the beginning and certainly a parable of the present. Christ is the cure!

———————

"And I will restore to you the years that the locust hath eaten, the cankerworm, and the caterpiller, and the palmerworm, my great army which I sent among you."

Joel 2:25

Some of man's hardest living is in the past. Don't worry about the wasted years. One good day with God will make up for it all. A day with the Lord is as a thousand years.

"For the Son of man is come to seek and to save that which was lost."

Luke 19:10

You have to get lost before you can be found. Self-sufficiency locks the Saviour out and makes a prisoner of the One who holds the key. "Behold, I stand at the door and knock."

"Who can understand his errors? cleanse thou me from secret faults."

Psalms 19:12

It is secret faults that keep us from Sacred thoughts. He, who is above all, knows what is underneath.

"Who can say, I have made my heart clean, I am pure from my sin?"

Proverbs 20:9

Can the rich, the poor, the educated, or the uneducated say it with authority? Can we, by our own goodness or deeds, make our hearts clean? No! Only through Christ can we have clean hearts and a good clean feeling between us and our fellow man.

"And he denied him, saying, Woman, I know him not."

Luke 22:57

If we expect Christ to stand up for us, we should speak out for Him. If we confess Him, He will also confess us before the Father and the Holy Angels.

"O earth, earth, earth, hear the word of the Lord."

Jeremiah 22:29

The need of our world is the same that it has ever been; more of God's Word, less of man's. "The word of the Lord endureth forever."

———————

"The Lord is my shepherd . . ."

Psalms 23:1

When the sheep get acquainted with the Shepherd, there is little else to worry about. "Acquaint now thyself with him, and be at peace."

———————

"But be ye doers of the word, and not hearers only, deceiving your own selves."

James 1:22

Personal application is the intended purpose of the Scriptures, yet we are so busy applying them to others, that we forget that they are also a remedy for what ails us.

———————

"And these shall go away into everlasting punishment: but the righteous into life eternal."
Matthew 25:46

The crossroads of life extend all the way into eternity. "Choose you this day whom ye will serve."

"And why take ye thought for raiment? Consider the lilies of the field, how they grow; they toil not, neither do they spin: and yet I say unto you, That even Solomon in all his glory was not arrayed like one of these."
Matthew 6:28,29

God's Spirit shining from within gives the greatest outward beauty.

"Faithful is he that calleth you, who also will do it."
I Thessalonians 5:24

Cheer up! God has His hand on you and is not going to leave you stranded. He who hath begun a good work in you will continue.

"And the Lord came, and stood, and called as at other times, Samuel, Samuel. Then Samuel answered, Speak; for thy servant heareth."

I Samuel 3:10

Whether you are a child or an adult, stay open to the call of God. Who knows what all He may have in store for you. Father, call multitudes into Your service, today. In Jesus' name. Amen.

"And ye shall know the truth, and the truth shall make you free."

John 8:32

It is the truth that turns us around and sets us free. "Jesus said, I am the way, the truth, and the life: no man cometh unto the Father, but by me." May this be the turning point and the liberation of multitudes in this moment, my Father, as they receive Your Son Jesus into their heart. In His name. Amen.

"For we brought nothing into this world, and it is certain we can carry nothing out."

I Timothy 6:7

Live only for the present, and you not only go out of this life empty-handed, but heavy-hearted. Make your life and means count for Christ.

―――――――――

"For God maketh my heart soft . . ."
Job 23:16

The man who has a mellow spirit will be respected by his fellow man and used of the Lord.

―――――――――

". . . I am come that they might have life, and that they might have it more abundantly."
John 10:10

Many are still content to live on worldly scraps in preference to a Heavenly supply. Are you living above the clouds or in them?

―――――――――

"Boast not thyself of tomorrow; for thou knowest not what a day may bring forth."
Proverbs 27:1

Many of our todays are spoiled by planning for tomorrows. "This is the day that the Lord hath made." Use it for His glory.

―――――――――

"As many as I love, I rebuke and chasten: be zealous therefore, and repent."

Revelation 3:19

We must constantly be monitoring our motives, lest we project self above the Saviour and works above worship.

———————

"Remember now thy Creator in the days of thy youth . . ."

Ecclesiastes 12:1

You can't give God what's left of life and expect His best. Give Him the best and the rest of your life.

———————

"Thou shalt not go up and down as a talebearer among thy people . . . I am the Lord."

Leviticus 19:16

Some people can't remember a good deed and can't forget a bad one.

———————

"I have no greater joy than to hear that my children walk in truth."

III John 4

Honest talk is good, if it is followed by honest walk. Truth is a terror to the unrighteous and a test to the righteous.

"But without faith it is impossible to please him: for he that cometh to God must believe that he is, and that he is a rewarder of them that diligently seek him."

Hebrews 11:6

This speaks of more than a casual communication with the Lord. Do you have time for that? You need to make time!

". . . The Lord is with you, while ye be with him; and if ye seek him, he will be found of you; but if ye forsake him, he will forsake you."

II Chronicles 15:2

The Lord is not in hiding. He is as close as your call. Father, may multitudes meet You, today, in Jesus' name. Amen.

"But be ye doers of the word, and not hearers only, deceiving your own selves."
James 1:22

The Word of God is meant to be taken in and walked out. You will never relive today. Make it a good one with God's help.

"The secret things belong unto the Lord our God: but those things which are revealed belong unto us and to our children forever, that we may do all the words of this law."
Deuteronomy 29:29

Look at the open-door policy for all of His promises. Father, give us a bold faith to claim what You have provided. In Jesus' name. Amen.

"Now unto him that is able to do exceeding abundantly above all that we ask or think, according to the power that worketh in us."
Ephesians 3:20

Release that power within you, and go on to victorious living. "Greater is he that is in you, than he that is in the world."

Inspirational Library

Beautiful purse/pocket-size editions of Christian classics bound in flexible leatherette. These books make thoughtful gifts for everyone on your list, including yourself!

When I'm on My Knees   The highly popular collection of devotional thoughts on prayer, especially for women.

Flexible Leatherette. $4.97

The Bible Promise Book   Over 1,000 promises from God's Word arranged by topic. What does God promise about matters like: Anger, Illness, Jealousy, Love, Money, Old Age, and Mercy? Find out in this book!

Flexible Leatherette. $3.97

Daily Wisdom for Women   A daily devotional for women seeking biblical wisdom to apply to their lives. Scripture taken from the New American Standard Version of the Bible.

Flexible Leatherette. $5.97

A Gentle Spirit   With an emphasis on personal spiritual development, this daily devotional for women draws from the best writings of Christian female authors.

Flexible Leatherette. $5.97

Available wherever books are sold.
Or order from:

Barbour Publishing, Inc.
P.O. Box 719
Uhrichsville, OH 44683
www.barbourbooks.com

If you order by mail, add $2.00 to your order for shipping.
Prices are subject to change without notice.